THE CONSCIOUS PARENT'S GUIDE TO

ADHD

A mindful approach for
helping your child gain focus
and self-control

Rebecca Branstetter, PhD

A adamsmedia
Avon, Massachusetts

DEDICATION

This book is dedicated to my supportive and wonderful husband, Steven.

Published by
Adams Media, a division of F+W Media, Inc.
57 Littlefield Street, Avon, MA 02322. U.S.A.
www.adamsmedia.com

Contains material adapted from *The Everything® Parent's Guide to ADHD in Children* by Carole Jacobs and Isadore Wendel, copyright © 2010 by F+W Media, Inc., ISBN 10: 1-60550-678-8, ISBN 13: 978-1-60550-678-4, and *The Everything® Parent's Guide to Raising Mindful Children* by Jeremy Wardle and Maureen Weinhardt, copyright © 2013 by F+W Media, Inc., ISBN 10: 1-4405-6130-0, ISBN 13: 978-1-4405-6130-6.

ISBN 10: 1-4405-9311-6
ISBN 13: 978-1-4405-9311-6
eISBN 10: 1-4405-9312-4
eISBN 13: 978-1-4405-9312-3

Printed in the United States of America.

10 9 8 7 6 5 4 3 2 1

Library of Congress Cataloging-in-Publication Data

Branstetter, Rebecca.
The conscious parent's guide to ADHD / Rebecca Branstetter, PhD.
    pages cm
  Includes index.
    ISBN 978-1-4405-9311-6 (pb) -- ISBN 1-4405-9311-6 (pb) -- ISBN 978-1-4405-9312-3 (ebook) -- ISBN 1-4405-9312-4 (ebook)
1. Attention-deficit hyperactivity disorder--Popular works. 2. Parent and child--Popular works. I. Title.
  RJ506.H9B724 2015
  618.92'8589--dc23
                    2015030421

This book is intended as general information only, and should not be used to diagnose or treat any health condition. In light of the complex, individual, and specific nature of health problems, this book is not intended to replace professional medical advice. The ideas, procedures, and suggestions in this book are intended to supplement, not replace, the advice of a trained medical professional. Consult your physician before adopting any of the suggestions in this book, as well as about any condition that may require diagnosis or medical attention. The author and publisher disclaim any liability arising directly or indirectly from the use of this book.

Many of the designations used by manufacturers and sellers to distinguish their products are claimed as trademarks. Where those designations appear in this book and F+W Media, Inc. was aware of a trademark claim, the designations have been printed with initial capital letters.

Cover design by Frank Rivera.

This book is available at quantity discounts for bulk purchases.
For information, please call 1-800-289-0963.

Contents

Introduction

Parenting a child with attention-deficit/hyperactivity disorder (ADHD) can be an exhausting, frustrating, bewildering, and overwhelming experience. In addition to managing day-to-day parenting challenges, parents may feel confused, stressed, and powerless when faced with the vast amount of information on ADHD. But as a parent, you can do a lot to help your child manage and control her symptoms, and to quiet the chaos that the disorder often imposes on families and marriages. It all begins with openness and patience, and a complete understanding of childhood ADHD.

Throughout this book you'll find tips for remaining flexible, calm, and mindful while taking the necessary steps to create a better future for your child. It is critical for parents to have effective tools for taking care of themselves and working positively with their kids. These mindfulness practices will provide tools for both you and your child to build a healthier, happier family household together.

The Conscious Parent's Guide to ADHD is a comprehensive resource for parents of children of all ages. It provides detailed information for recognizing and managing your child's disorder from preschool through high school. This guide offers practical advice on the telltale signs and symptoms of childhood ADHD and information on getting a reliable diagnosis, evaluation, and treatment for your child.

By reading this book, you'll glean the basic medical knowledge necessary to talk intelligently about your child's condition to his doctor. You'll also learn about the condition's classic symptoms, diagnostic and evaluation techniques, and an increasingly sophisticated arsenal of high-tech treatment and medication modalities used to treat childhood ADHD.

Although almost all children have days when they don't complete their homework, blurt out the wrong things in class, or forget where they put their backpacks, those days are the norm, rather than the exception, for children with ADHD. As you'll learn by reading *The Conscious Parent's Guide to ADHD*, not every child has the same ADHD symptoms, and a child's symptoms may change over time. Some children with ADHD are hyperactive; others are quiet dreamers who stare into space, miles away from their teachers and homework at hand. Still others are so impulsive that they butt into every conversation, are overly blunt and tactless, or invade everyone's space.

The Conscious Parent's Guide to ADHD will also help remove any blame, shame, or guilt you may be harboring about having caused or contributed to your child's disorder. You'll learn that your child's ADHD was not caused by bad parenting, by eating a poor diet, or by watching too much television, but that it is a neurobiological disorder caused by biochemical imbalances in the brain. Scientists now believe that childhood ADHD is not one single disorder, but a cluster of disorders that affect different parts of the brain. Researchers also know that childhood ADHD is a genetic disorder. That means if you or your spouse have ADHD, your children are at a higher risk of developing it, too.

Although there's no cure to date for childhood ADHD, perhaps the best news about this disorder is that most of your child's symptoms can be successfully managed and controlled through a combination of medication and therapy.

It's not easy for parents or children to live with childhood ADHD. Early intervention won't cure your child's disorder, but it can dramatically improve his chances of managing his ADHD symptoms and doing well academically and emotionally. In fact, studies show that most children with ADHD can be successfully diagnosed and treated and go on to lead more productive lives.

Finally, *The Conscious Parent's Guide to ADHD* will give you practical tools for coping with the challenges of parenting, while being present and mindful of the joyful moments with your child. Mindfulness practice, which is the art of being present in a nonjudgmental way, has been a hot topic in scientific research for a number of years. Evidence continues to mount demonstrating that mindfulness helps parents and children alike deal with stress and negative emotions, improve focus, enhance happiness, and improve cognitive and executive functioning skills. By learning, modeling, and teaching mindfulness practices in your family, both you and your child will have a new set of tools for success now and in the future.

The key to your child getting and staying well is parental knowledge and awareness. By picking up this book, you've made a commitment to learn as much as you can about childhood ADHD and taken the first step in your and your child's journey to improved health and happiness.

CHAPTER 1

Conscious Parenting

Being a conscious parent is all about building strong, sustainable bonds with your children through mindful living and awareness. Traditional power-based parenting techniques that promote compliance and obedience can disconnect you from your children. Conscious parenting, on the other hand, helps you develop a positive emotional connection with your child. You acknowledge your child's unique self and attempt to empathize with his way of viewing the world. Through empathetic understanding and tolerance you create a safe environment where your child feels his ideas and concerns are truly being heard. When you find yourself in a stressful situation with your child, rather than reacting with anger or sarcasm, conscious parenting reminds you to instead take a step back, reflect, and look for a peaceful solution—one that honors your child's individuality and motivations. This approach benefits all children, especially those with ADHD. Your child with ADHD has much to offer in the form of gifts and talents. Adopting the conscious parent philosophy can relieve your stress and improve your child's self-image.

The Benefits of Conscious Parenting

It is important to note that conscious parenting is not a set of rules or regulations that you must follow, but rather it is a system of beliefs. Conscious parents engage and connect with their children, using mindful and positive discipline rather than punishment. They try to be present when they're spending time with their children, avoiding distractions such as TV and social media. Conscious parents respect their children and accept them as they are. The most important part of conscious parenting is building an emotional connection with your child so you can understand the underlying reasons for his behavior.

Conscious parenting is about listening with full attention, and embracing a nonjudgmental acceptance of yourself and your child. As you engage in the act of *becoming*, you will discover a heightened sense of emotional awareness of yourself and your child, a clearer self-regulation in the parenting relationship, and a greater compassion for yourself and your child.

Conscious parenting brings with it a number of benefits including improved communication, stronger relationships, and the feeling of greater happiness and satisfaction in life. Some of these benefits appear quickly, whereas others take some time to emerge. The benefits of conscious parenting and mindfulness are a result of making them part of your daily life. With practice, conscious parenting becomes an integral part of who and how you are in the world, and will in turn become a central part of who your child is as well.

AWARENESS

One of the first benefits of conscious parenting that you (and your child) will see is a heightened awareness of yourself and your inner life, including your emotions, thoughts, and feelings. As you become more aware of these various forces moving within you, you can begin to watch them rise without being at their mercy. For example, when you are aware that you are becoming angry, you have a choice about whether to act from that anger or attend to that feeling directly.

> Mindfulness is the practice of being attentive in every moment, and noticing what is taking place both inside and outside of you without judgment. It is the practice of purposefully seeing your thoughts, emotions, experiences, and surroundings as they arise. Simply put, mindfulness is the act of paying attention.

As you become more skilled at noticing the thoughts and feelings that arise, you will begin to notice them more quickly, maybe even before they start to affect your actions. This awareness is itself a powerful tool. It opens up the possibility to say, "Hey, I'm pretty mad right now . . . " as opposed to yelling at somebody you care about because you were upset about something else. It can do exactly the same thing for your child, helping her to learn to communicate about her feelings rather than just reacting from that place of emotion. As with most things, children learn this best by seeing it modeled by the adults in their lives.

WELL-BEING

Conscious parents understand that all they do and say over the course of each day *matters*. Mindfulness is a sense of the *now*, being in the present, in the moment without regard or worry for the past or future. When

> Each human being possesses the tools for contributing something of value. Assess your gifts and talents—those personality traits and skills that make you unique—and determine how to employ them to enhance your parenting. If you take a full accounting of yourself—good, bad, and indifferent—and *own* the sum total of your individual experience, you are taking the first step toward conscious parenting.

you become more mindful, you may find that you become more accepting of the things in life that you can't change and experience less stress. The net result is greater satisfaction and enjoyment of whatever each day has to offer. This sense of well-being offers a satisfaction and contentment in knowing that we are who we are intended to be, doing precisely what we are designed for in the moment.

Giving Your Child Full Attention

Conscious parenting can be an amazing antidote to counteract any negative projections and perceptions you or your child might experience. As a conscious parent, you can create a positive, nonjudgmental, and loving environment that your child can count on. With the emotional connections that you form with your child, you celebrate your child as an individual, with a unique personality. You let your child know that you understand his behavior as a reaction to the way that he exists in the world.

Negative thoughts and feelings should be shed in favor of positive perspectives. Your child is a child, first and foremost. A beautiful, entirely unique, magnificently gorgeous human being with faults and frailties as well as gifts and talents; the same is true of everyone.

In childhood, your son or daughter will rely upon you and your family to provide a solid foundation of self-esteem. Equipped with a strong sense of self-worth, your child will be better prepared to enter into a life that will likely present many challenges. Much of your time and energy will be expended in raising, counseling, and disciplining your child in ways that she will understand. It is important to try to equalize those occasions by reinforcing your love and appreciation of her gifts and talents.

Instead of feeling worn out by your child's intense interests, take a moment to indulge him and listen carefully. Or, catch your child doing something amazingly gifted and praise him lavishly. Your outpouring of attention and genuine interest will come back to you tenfold.

UNDERSTANDING PARENT TRAINING

An important part of treatment for a child with ADHD is parent training. Children with ADHD may not respond to the usual parenting practices, so experts recommend parent education. This approach has been successful in educating parents on how to help their children develop better organizational skills, problem-solving skills, and how to cope with their ADHD symptoms.

Parent training can be conducted in groups or with individual families and is offered by therapists or in special classes. The national organization CHADD (Children and Adults with Attention-Deficit/Hyperactivity Disorder) offers a unique education program to help parents and individuals navigate the challenges of ADHD across their lifespans. Find more information about CHADD's "Parent to Parent" program by visiting CHADD's website at *www.chadd.org*.

MINDFULNESS PRACTICE FOR PARENTS

Recently, parenting groups have begun to incorporate "Mindfulness Practices" into their parent education and support groups. Parenting a child with ADHD can be very stressful, as traditional parenting tools do not always work, and you may sometimes feel a tinge of judgment from others (and from yourself!) about parenting skills. This is where conscious parenting can help.

The practice of mindfulness is being aware of the present moment—the thoughts, feelings, and sensations—and not judging them harshly or filtering them through a biased lens. This nonjudgmental awareness is then used as a tool to consider and make more conscious parenting decisions. Chapter 8 focuses on mindfulness tools for parents and children. A wealth of information about mindfulness and mindful parenting can also be found at *www.mindful.org*.

Understanding the Symptoms of ADHD

Trying to understand the symptoms of ADHD can be overwhelming. To get the whole picture, it's best to start with the origins of ADHD. In 1980, psychiatrists decided to reclassify ADHD as two separate subsets. One was attention deficit disorder with hyperactivity, or ADD–H. The other was attention deficit disorder without hyperactivity, or ADD with no "H." After further study, researchers realized hyperactivity/impulsivity was actually a larger problem than inattention, and decided to change the name of the disorder to reflect their findings.

The symptom of inattention in childhood ADHD actually refers to a whole galaxy of attention problems, not just a lack of attention. Your child could also be so focused on one thing that she can't pay attention to anything else. Or she may not be able to decide what to focus on, how to maintain her attention, or how to shift her focus when necessary.

In 1987, the disorder was renamed attention-deficit/hyperactivity disorder, or ADHD, and reclassified as a disorder with not two, but three distinct subsets: inattentive, hyperactive/impulsive, and combined type (children who display both inattentive and hyperactive/impulsive symptoms). For the purpose of this book, the disorder will be called childhood ADHD to comply with current psychiatric terminology.

The "predominantly inattentive presentation" is for children with attention deficits but no problems with hyperactivity. The "predominantly hyperactive/impulsive presentation" diagnosis is used for hyperactive children, who may also be impulsive. The "combined presentation" is for children with both inattentive and hyperactive/impulsive behaviors.

Adolescents and adults may outgrow or overcome their symptoms. If so, they are diagnosed as being "in partial remission." This reflects the new view that people do not outgrow the disorder, but may learn to compensate so that the symptoms are not disabling. There is also a catch-all diagnosis for children who don't meet the standard criteria. If they don't have enough symptoms or their symptoms aren't severe enough, they can be diagnosed with a nonspecific form of ADHD.

What is the benefit of being diagnosed with ADHD? There are two reasons a diagnosis is helpful. First, a diagnosis can help you get a better handle on the nature of your child's difficulties and help you understand the next steps based on the years of research on ADHD. Secondly, a diagnosis may open up doors to interventions, supports, and services that would otherwise be unavailable to you and your child.

Predominantly Inattentive Presentation

Many people used to refer to the "predominantly inattentive presentation" of attention-deficit/hyperactivity disorder simply as ADD. Symptoms include:

O Difficulty listening, even when being directly addressed

O Trouble continuing to pay attention to activities involving either work or play

O Difficulty paying attention to details and avoiding careless mistakes

O Problems completing tasks, chores, and assignments

O Difficulty organizing activities and tasks

O Trouble doing tasks that require sustained mental effort, such as required for schoolwork

O Difficulty keeping track of possessions and materials, such as toys, clothes, homework papers, and school supplies

O Being easily distracted

O Difficulty remembering things

In order for his symptoms to be considered bona fide, it should be clear that a child cannot sustain attention and cannot concentrate on mental tasks for extended periods. Problems stemming from boredom, disinterest, lack of motivation, and defiance are not supposed to be counted as ADHD symptoms—though they often are.

It is easy to see why attention deficits create problems in school. Students with short attention spans cannot concentrate on schoolwork for the long periods required to do their work. Being easily distracted poses a major problem in crowded classrooms, which are filled with continuous rustles and murmurs. If students' attention wanders at unpredictable moments, they miss portions of lectures and don't hear explanations about assignments and tests.

You may notice lapses of attention when you give your child directions and instructions, which can result in considerable frustration and upset at home. You might send your child to clean up his room and later discover him playing with baseball cards instead of doing his chore. If this happens, remind yourself to be calm, and simply begin a dialogue with your child regarding his actions. Ask him if he remembers what you asked him to do in his room, and follow his train of thought. If the child's attention strayed while you were giving instructions, the youngster might have understood that he was to go to his room but missed what he was expected to do when he arrived. Or, after going to his room to clean it, he might have seen his box of baseball cards and spent an hour going through them without giving another thought to what he was supposed to do.

Poor organizational skills can cause a host of problems in school and at home. Many children get confused during projects and tasks to the point that they don't know how to proceed.

Some youngsters become upset and cry over seemingly simple homework assignments and chores, claiming they don't know how to do them. If parents and teachers are convinced that a youngster is bright enough and possesses the skills needed to do the work, they may conclude that the child is overly emotional.

Other youngsters don tough-guy masks and display an "I couldn't care less" attitude, so it is hard for adults to recognize that poor organization is at the heart of many of their children's problems. The solution may be to break long assignments and projects into a number of small steps and have students complete them one at a time. Whatever you choose, remember to respect your child's process.

Predominantly Hyperactive Presentation

The second type of attention-deficit/hyperactivity disorder, which includes hyperactivity and impulsiveness, is technically known as the "predominantly hyperactive presentation." Most people refer to it simply as ADHD.

For this type, children's difficulties must stem from hyperactivity or from a combination of hyperactive and impulsive behaviors. *The Diagnostic and Statistical Manual of Mental Disorders, Fifth Edition (DSM-5)* lists six symptoms of hyperactive behavior and three symptoms of impulsive behavior. A child must have six out of the nine symptoms to be diagnosed with the predominantly hyperactive type. Teens and adults (over age seventeen) must have five of the nine characteristics.

The Diagnostic and Statistical Manual of Mental Disorders, Fifth Edition (DSM-5), which was published by the American Psychiatric Association in 2013, is a list of mental and behavior disorders recognized by doctors in the United States.

SYMPTOMS OF HYPERACTIVITY

Hyperactive children have an energy level that their parents and teachers consider excessive. They may appear to be driven by a powerful motor, so that they continue to wiggle even when at rest. Symptoms include:

O Squirming and fidgeting even when seated

O Getting up when expected to remain seated

O Running excessively and climbing in inappropriate situations

O Difficulty playing quietly

O Being always on the go

O Talking excessively

Stay present with your child, and try to identify possible symptoms of hyperactivity in her daily routine. Some children squirm and fidget while sitting at their school desks, while watching television at home, and while listening to bedtime stories. Hyperactive adolescents may swing their legs, tap their feet, drum their fingers on their desk, pop their chewing gum, or chew their fingernails. They are likely to report that they feel restless much of the time. Some say that when they must remain seated for more than a few minutes, they feel as though they're about to jump out of their skin.

Recent studies have shown that kids with ADHD did better on working memory tasks (such as solving a math problem) when they were allowed to move around, whereas kids without ADHD did poorer on such tasks.

Professionals believe that ADHD sufferers share a common problem: They require much more stimulation to remain attentive than the average youngster. As anyone who has sat through a long sermon or attempted to read a book she finds boring knows the mind must have enough stimulation to remain attentive.

HYPERFOCUS

Despite their short attention spans and inability to pay attention in school, children with ADHD can concentrate on a video game or television program so well that they don't even notice when someone is standing two feet away, yelling for their attention. Most parents find this extremely irritating. They think their children are defiant, pointing out that they concentrate and sit still well enough "when they want to."

When children diagnosed with ADHD are fully engaged in a highly stimulating activity such as a television program or interactive game, they become so attentive that they cannot readily shift their attention away from it. Do the minds of children diagnosed with ADHD move at the same speed as a fast-action video game or rock video? This seems to be a possibility.

Researchers have found that a sluggish reward circuit in the brains of children with ADHD makes otherwise interesting tasks seem mundane or boring. Children with ADHD need a higher level of reward or interest to sustain attention. Video games and other high-reward and stimulating activities seem to fit the bill, and this is why children with ADHD may have no problems focusing for hours on such activities.

IMPULSIVITY

Many children with ADHD also have impulsivity. Impulsive children have difficulty inhibiting the urge to act or speak and often seem unable to contain themselves. Doctors look for three main signs:

O Blurting answers before the teacher or parent has finished asking the question

O Not waiting his turn

O Interrupting conversations or intruding into other's activities

Impulsive children reach for fragile objects despite repeated reminders not to touch. They grab other children's toys without asking permission. At school, they get up to sharpen their pencils the moment they determine the tips are dull or broken, without waiting to ask permission.

Peers dislike having other students disrupt the classroom, interrupt their conversations, and intrude in their games, so impulsive children often have social difficulties. Some impulsive children alienate others because they have hair-trigger tempers and are quick to take affront.

Primary and Secondary Symptoms

Although childhood ADHD is characterized by the three primary symptoms of hyperactivity, inattention, and impulsivity, your child may also exhibit many secondary symptoms. For many children, secondary symptoms are more problematic than the core symptoms of ADHD. As a conscious parent, it is best to talk to your child when you see these secondary symptoms pop up. Staying present with your child can help you identify when he is at risk for developing harmful symptoms, and can help you refocus his attention on bettering himself.

Here are just a few of the typical secondary symptoms suffered by children with ADHD:

- Anticipating failure. Because many children have a habit of repeated failures, whether it's losing things, forgetting their homework, being late, or losing track of their thoughts, they suffer a great deal of anxiety over expecting to fail.

- Excessive worrying. Often accompanied by anxiety and restlessness, children with ADHD worry about anything and everything. The worry often makes them appear detached or disinterested.

- Boredom. Children with ADHD are easily bored and often need continual stimulation, change, and even conflict. Getting bored also makes them prone to high-risk behavior, such as smoking, drug abuse, and promiscuity.

- Frustration. Children with ADHD are easily frustrated and impatient with themselves and others, often over the smallest things. They also tend to have short, explosive tempers.

- Low self-esteem. Children with ADHD are frequently criticized and blamed for their shortcomings, at home, at school, or in social situations. Years of feeling as if they haven't measured up erodes their self-esteem and confidence.

- Insomnia or sleep disturbances. Many children with ADHD have trouble falling asleep and/or staying asleep. Causes range from hyperactivity and restlessness to side effects from stimulant medications.

○ Alcohol and substance abuse. Some adolescents and teens with ADHD use drugs and alcohol to numb their feelings of frustration and low self-esteem. Others use alcohol and drugs because they are drawn to daring or risky behavior.

Important Points to Consider

Conscious parenting is a *process* that is as unique and individual as each family is unique. Parenting in a mindful manner comes with an authentic appreciation for your gifts and talents (and those of your child), as well as an understanding for how best to employ those gifts and talents to help your child grow to be a happy, successful member of society. Think of this style of raising your child as *parenting with grace*.

Having a gracious approach means understanding the following:

1. There is safety in sameness and comfort in what is familiar.

2. In order to feel safe and comfortable, the child must have control.

3. Think about the times when your child appeared most content, comfortable, and at ease. Was he enjoying playing a solitary computer game? Was he alone in his bedroom, drawing whales and sharks? Or was he directing the play of his siblings and friends? In these instances, was your child engaged in a favored, pleasurable activity? Was it a repetitive activity from which he derived comfort? And during this activity, did your child have control? The response to these questions is likely yes.

4. Now, reverse the situations and remove the elements of safety, comfort, and control. Say the computer unexpectedly locks up and the video game is interrupted. A sibling won't turn down his music while your child is attempting to concentrate on the details of his marine life drawings. Or a friend decides she doesn't want to be "bossed" by your child and opts out of their playtime. These situations are unexpected and unpredictable. Your child feels unsafe, uncomfortable, and out of control when the unpredictable occurs and wins out.

5. Your child may feel overwhelmed by the loss of control. He may act out in a variety of undesirable ways. But if you take a moment to understand what's going on, you'll realize that he has good reasons for his behavior and is doing the best he knows how in order to cope with the loss of safety and comfort. His reaction is a logical progression of that escalation until he learns other coping strategies. When you are present in your parenting, you understand this and you can communicate your understanding to your child. Your emotional attachment to your child means that you can let your child know that you understand *why* he is behaving in a certain way, even as you work together to find a better way of reacting the next time.

6. Your recognition of ADHD as a positive attribute and your appreciation of your child's gifts and talents will make your home and family a place where he feels unconditionally loved and understood. Many parents just like you have made this mindful-parenting commitment and can readily attest to the profound, loving impact it has made on their lives.

CHAPTER 2

Getting a Diagnosis

Many parents don't know where to begin when they suspect their children have ADHD. It is a very overwhelming process that tests your patience and composure. Being a conscious parent means taking pause before you act or lose your cool. Understand that the situation you are in is difficult, but not impossible. Unlike diseases and conditions that can be easily diagnosed by getting a blood test or an x-ray, there is no one simple test that confirms the presence of ADHD. For most parents, getting the right diagnosis for their children usually entails going through a series of assessments from one or more medical professionals. Most experts believe that the best diagnostic and treatment plan is a multidisciplinary approach that involves a team of medical and ADHD experts.

Where Should You Start?

The choice of where to start your search can be bewildering, especially considering that different medical specialists have different strengths and are qualified to do different things. For instance, both psychiatrists and psychologists treat mental disorders, but most psychologists cannot prescribe medication or medical tests and must refer patients to someone else for those.

Further complicating matters is the fact that methods of evaluating children for ADHD are not as scientific as most people assume. There are no medical tests for this condition. Because children's behavior typically improves in unfamiliar, smaller, and structured environments such as waiting rooms and examining offices, doctors do not expect to personally witness the behavior problems that are of concern. Many rely exclusively on information provided by a parent or teacher.

It can be hard to keep calm and not become frustrated when you are facing these hurdles. You aren't alone. Many conscious parents feel the same way. Try to focus your attention on staying in the moment with your child. When you feel yourself beginning to get too stressed out, take a few minutes to get in touch with your emotions and to evaluate why you feel the way you do.

Common Diagnostic Challenges of Childhood ADHD

Although virtually every child will show ADHD-like symptoms from time to time, the requirements for a standard ADHD diagnosis are quite stringent. Besides having enough symptoms of attention deficits, hyperactivity, and/or impulsiveness, signs of these problems must have been present early in childhood—at least before age twelve. A child might not have been evaluated by a professional until after that age, however the developmental history must indicate that the behavior was present early in life.

In addition, the current troublesome behavior must have been present for at least six months. Behavior problems that have been going on for shorter periods are more likely to be reactions to a specific trauma or life change, such as the birth of a sibling or a family move.

SYMPTOMS PRESENT IN SEVERAL SETTINGS

To be considered symptoms of ADHD, the behavior in question must be more frequent as well as more severe than is typical for youngsters at the same level of development. Children must have serious behavior problems in two or more important settings (e.g. at home, at school, with peers) for a standard ADHD diagnosis.

Behavior problems that are limited to home are more likely to stem from family stress, poor parenting, or difficult family dynamics. If students have problems at school but get along well in other environments, this usually suggests they are struggling with teaching or learning difficulties.

My child keeps getting in trouble at school. Could she have ADHD? If she is doing well in other settings, the first step is to find out if there is a problem at school that needs attention. Everything from being bullied to having an especially strict or permissive teacher can cause children to act up. Set up a meeting with your child's school to rule out situational factors that may be causing problems.

Problems that are confined to the playground and unsupervised playtime in the neighborhood suggest problems coping with unstructured situations, or having a personality trait known as risk-taking or thrill-seeking. People with this trait require more stimulation to avoid boredom, and they are drawn to activities that most youngsters would view as overly dangerous or frightening.

Diagnostic Considerations The standard ADHD diagnosis requires "clear evidence" of "significant impairment in social, academic, or occupational functioning," in addition to the child having serious difficulty managing in several environments, according to the *DSM-5*. Impaired social functioning might mean that the child cannot make or keep friends because of her off-putting behavior.

For the standard (as opposed to "unspecified") ADHD diagnosis, a child must have many specific symptoms reflecting difficulty with attention, hyperactivity, and impulsivity. In addition, the problems must have started before age twelve, and they must be pervasive and severe. However, a child can be diagnosed with a "specified" or "unspecified" attention-deficit/hyperactivity disorder (ADHD) with just a few symptoms that only create problems in one setting and that started later in life. The *DSM-5* indicates that these diagnoses are even appropriate for children with behavior patterns marked by sluggishness, daydreaming, and hypoactivity or low energy level, sometimes referred to as "sluggish cognitive tempo." Many combinations of problematic behaviors can now be diagnosed under the umbrella term of ADHD.

The "sluggish cognitive tempo" presentation of ADHD is not an officially recognized disorder by the *DSM-5*. However, research is showing more and more that it may be a distinct disorder that warrants its own diagnostic label.

It is okay to be confused about the diagnostic criteria for ADHD. Even professionals struggle with finding the correct diagnostic label. To begin your journey in mindful parenting, just notice and acknowledge the confusion and do not judge it as "good" or "bad."

How to Find a Specialist

The best way to locate a specialist to do an ADHD evaluation is to contact your child's pediatrician or a child guidance clinic for a referral. Ask if there are any clinics specializing in ADHD in your area. The tests your child needs cut across a number of specialties, and a clinic is likely to house most of the professionals under one roof.

However, clinics specifically designed to evaluate and treat ADHD are few and far between, so most families use their child's physician, a psychologist, or a psychiatrist to coordinate the referrals to various specialists, compile all of the test results, pull together the recommendations, and conduct checkups after treatment has begun.

Support groups can serve as an informal clearinghouse of information on recommended physicians, specialists, and treatments in your area, and may also offer you and your child the moral support you both need. To find one near you, talk to ADHD specialists, local universities, or the national organization of Children and Adults with Attention-Deficit/ Hyperactivity Disorder at *www.chadd.org*.

TYPES OF SPECIALISTS WHO TREAT ADHD

For a comprehensive evaluation, many professionals need to be involved. They may include:

- MD (medical doctor) or DO (doctor of osteopathic medicine)
- Child psychologist
- Child psychiatrist
- School psychologist
- Neurologist
- Audiologist
- Educational diagnostician
- Allergist
- Clinical nutritionist (licensed by the Clinical Nutrition Certification Board)

Any state-licensed physician or psychologist can legally diagnose and treat ADHD. Psychiatrists are physicians and can prescribe medication. Psychologists specialize in psychological testing. (Both may also provide counseling and psychotherapy.) Psychologists do not prescribe medication in most states, although this is changing. Sometimes licensed educational diagnosticians/psychologists and qualified school psychologists can diagnose disorders and make treatment recommendations, but they do not usually provide treatment.

If you are in need of a new physician, a doctor of osteopathic medicine (DO) may be a good choice. Like other physicians, DOs attend medical school, but their curriculum places more emphasis on preventative, family, and community medicine. DOs prescribe medication and perform surgeries, but tend to be broader in their approach and more concerned with holistic healing. Be sure to ask if the doctor works with children before scheduling an appointment.

OTHER SPECIALISTS WHO TREAT CHILDHOOD ADHD

Many other types of specialists diagnose and help treat childhood ADHD and may be able to offer additional assistance with assessment, coping skills, behavior modification, and problem solving. Part of being a conscious parent is being open and honest about your child's struggle. Enlisting the help of various professionals may help you understand your child's behavior now and in the future.

O Neuropsychologists are trained in the biological and neurological basis of thinking and learning. They may use a battery of tests to measure cognitive and behavior functioning. Neuropsychologists are usually less expensive than psychiatrists, but more expensive than psychologists.

O Neurologists are medical doctors who specialize in diagnosing and treating diseases and disorders of the brain and nervous system. Neurologists may be able to differentiate between symptoms of childhood ADHD and overlapping conditions such as seizure disorder or brain injury. They can also prescribe medications and medical tests. They tend to be very expensive.

O Psychiatric nurse practitioners and nurse practitioners, or ARNPs, are generally well trained and knowledgeable about the diagnosis and treatment of ADHD. They are usually less expensive and more available than medical professionals, and may be helpful with life management skills.

- Registered nurses, or RNs, may also be able to make an initial diagnosis and offer assistance with life skills. As with psychiatric nurses, they can't prescribe medical testing and medication and must refer patients to other medical professionals. However, they are usually less expensive and easier to schedule than psychologists or psychiatrists.

- Master and doctoral level counselors have advanced degrees in psychology or counseling, but they are not medical doctors. They can do an initial assessment and help your child deal with a wide variety of everyday life skills and problems. However, they must refer your child to a doctor or another professional for medication and medical testing. They may also provide services such as neurofeedback and biofeedback.

- Individual, group, family, and marriage counselors and therapists can provide you, your spouse, your family, and your child with help in dealing with specific issues such as getting along in social settings, functioning at work, parenting, organizational issues at home, and dealing with childhood ADHD-related problems in relationships and marriage.

- Social workers are usually employed by public or private healthcare agencies to offer counseling to people served by the agency. Treatment is generally affordable. Although social workers may be able to offer an initial diagnosis, they may lack the training necessary to distinguish between the symptoms of childhood ADHD and overlapping conditions such as clinical depression, anxiety, or bipolar disorder. Social workers can't prescribe medications or medical tests.

- School psychologists are employed by the public schools to assess students for disabilities that fall under special education law in order to make educational recommendations. Like social workers, they may be able to offer an initial diagnosis, but they may not be able to rule in or out overlapping conditions. They cannot prescribe medication, though they can provide school supports and coaching for you, your child, and your child's teacher(s). Their services are free.

○ ADHD coaches specialize in helping children and teenagers manage everyday problems and situations, such as organization, time management, memory, follow-through, and motivation. Unlike psychiatrists and psychologists, they don't counsel. Instead, they address the present, using an approach that asks children and teenagers to focus on where they are now, where they want to be, and how they can get there. Although generally less expensive than psychologists, coaches aren't cheap. Many coaches request that your child commit to four to six hourly sessions over several weeks or months. Fees range anywhere from $75 an hour and up, and are not typically covered by health insurance.

Unlike doctors, coaches are not licensed by regulatory boards, nor are they required to undergo special training or licensing to practice. For this reason, some medical and psychological professionals question the validity of coaching as supplemental therapy. For more information on accredited coaches in your area, visit the International Coach Federation website at *www .coachfederation.org.*

Importance of Medical Examination

If your family physician has known your child since he was born, it may be easier for her to arrive at a diagnosis than for a physician who has never met your child before. Either way, any diagnosis for childhood ADHD should begin with a complete medical examination to rule out other diseases and disorders that may be masquerading as childhood ADHD.

As an MD, your family physician can also order the necessary medical tests and procedures your child may require, as well as prescribe prescription drugs. It may be easier to get in to see your family physician than to get an appointment with a specialist who doesn't know you or your child. Your family physician is also likely to charge less than some specialists.

Getting a medical checkup with your family doctor is a very good place to start if you suspect your child has ADHD. Family physicians are becoming increasingly aware of childhood ADHD, however, your family physician may not have expertise or experience in diagnosing and treating the condition. In addition, she may not be comfortable diagnosing a condition in which a common treatment is the long-term use of a stimulant medication.

Help Your Doctor Develop a History of Behavior

No matter what type of specialist your child sees first, an important first step in the evaluation process is for you, your child, and your child's doctor to work together to collect background information and take a detailed developmental history. The goal of a personal history is to ascertain the exact nature of the behavior problems, determine that they have been present for at least six months, establish that they occur in multiple settings, identify any special stresses your child has been under, find out what has been done at school and at home to try to help, and ensure that another diagnosis does not better explain the difficulties.

To prepare for your first interview with a physician, collect your youngster's medical and school records and take them with you to the appointment unless your doctor requests them in advance. If you have recorded in a baby book information about the age at which your child first sat up alone, walked, talked, etc., be sure to bring it with you as well.

Your physician will also want to interview you about your family medical history, and find out if anyone else in the family has ADHD, which is believed to be a hereditary condition. This is where having a solid emotional bond with your child can help. Having a trusting relationship between you, your child, and his doctor can make the diagnostic process a bit easier.

Your child's doctor may ask her teachers to fill out an evaluation form for your child. Often the evaluations are mailed to the school before the first appointment so the doctor can review the information in advance.

Classroom teachers are usually the first to urge parents to seek an ADHD evaluation. Because they work with so many students, teachers have a better basis than parents for judging whether behavior is typical. Because teachers are less emotionally involved, they also tend to be more objective than parents.

Parents should also complete a checklist of problem behavior. Although parents and teachers tend to report different problems on the behavior checklists, they usually agree that the youngster's behavior is difficult, trying, and frustrating.

Tests Your Doctor May Use

Children with ADHD symptoms are typically prescribed a battery of medical tests. A neurological evaluation is important, as petit mal seizures can cause "spaciness" and lapses of attention. Thyroid problems can cause children's activity levels to be abnormally high or low, and can cause inattentiveness. Some practitioners may also test for lead poisoning, allergies, and nutritional deficiencies, although there is no scientific evidence linking these factors to ADHD.

HEARING TESTS
Children should have their hearing checked. Middle ear infections can be so minor that there is no fever, but the combination of muffled sounds and feeling under the weather can make children distracted, inattentive, and irritable. An audiologist should investigate the possibility of language-processing problems. If the child passes all of those tests, it is time for a psychological evaluation and educational testing.

MENTAL HEALTH SCREENING
Children should be screened for other emotional and mental disorders before a diagnosis is made. Depression, anxiety, and stress reactions

("post-traumatic stress disorder") cause difficulties with sustaining attention and produce agitation that can look so much like hyperactivity, even seasoned professionals cannot tell them apart. Moreover, almost two-thirds of children diagnosed with ADHD also have another psychological, behavior, or learning disorder.

PSYCHOLOGICAL EVALUATION

If mental health screening suggests that a child has another psychological problem in addition to or instead of ADHD, further evaluation by a psychologist, psychiatrist, or another credentialed mental health provider is in order.

A psychological evaluation involves taking a psychosocial history by interviewing parents in order to identify current and past individual, family, and social problems. Trauma from parental divorce, abandonment, alcoholism, abuse, domestic violence, and stress from chronic family tension can cause ADHD symptoms and other psychological, behavior, and learning problems.

Older children are then interviewed at length and younger children are observed in a playroom. Children ages six to twelve typically undergo a combination of interviews and playroom observations. If the interviews and observations suggest a need for further evaluation, the next step is likely to be psychological testing.

A complete psychological evaluation includes personality, intelligence, neuropsychological, and educational testing. A school psychologist or educational diagnostician employed by the school district may be legally obligated to administer some or even all of the tests, which relieves the family of this financial burden.

Educational Testing

Students diagnosed with ADHD should undergo educational and intelligence testing. The required tests can be administered by the psychologist during the psychological evaluation or by a qualified educational diagnostician or school psychologist. Learning disabilities are rampant among children with ADHD, so there is a good chance that special education services will be helpful.

Moreover, students with severe learning problems often misbehave in school or simply stop paying attention because they are frustrated and overwhelmed by the work. They act up at home because they are upset about their inability to succeed academically. Their ADHD symptoms disappear once they receive instruction targeted to their particular learning style and needs.

The same applies to students who are especially academically advanced, except that their inattention, frustration, and classroom behavior problems are more likely to stem from boredom. They settle down and their concentration improves when they are given more challenging work. Educational testing can often pinpoint issues that are causing children to misbehave.

Is This Specialist Right for Your Child?

Finding the right medical team for childhood ADHD is probably going to require more time and effort on your part than trying to find a doctor to set a broken leg. This is especially true if you feel you've already wasted a lot of time and money on specialists and treatments that didn't help. Taking a mindful and open approach to meeting new doctors can help you evaluate whether they will be helpful for your son or daughter. This doesn't mean you have to continue seeing them, but be willing to hear their perspectives.

Here are ten things to consider in selecting a specialist:

1. Has the specialist in question been recommended by friends or family members with childhood ADHD, members of your support group, medical experts, or other people or professionals you already admire, respect, and trust?

2. Does the specialist have the requisite academic and professional credentials and experience, as well as a proven track record in treating children with ADHD? This includes being a member in good standing of national boards and professional organizations devoted to psychiatry, psychology, etc.

3. Is he informed about the latest medications, treatments, therapies, diagnostic tools, and tests for childhood ADHD?

4. Is he open to exploring new medications and alternative approaches that you've always wanted to explore, or is he inflexible and stuck in his ways?

5. Do you and your child like the specialist enough to sense your child can hang in there for the duration, and/or when the going gets tough?

6. During your first meeting, did your specialist do as much listening as talking, or did you and your child have trouble getting a word in edgewise?

7. Does the specialist seem to "get" your child and regard him as a unique human being, or do you get the feeling he's already pegged your child as Type 1, 2, or 3 on the basis of a short test or conversation?

8. Can you afford to see the specialist regularly without emptying your bank account?

9. Is your specialist someone you think your child can easily fool? For example, can he see through little white lies, sins of omission, exaggerations, misleading statements, or false bravado your child might be tempted to use?

10. Will your specialist be there for your child when things get difficult? Or would he be more likely to write your child off, and send you a bill?

Scoring: If you answered "yes" to questions 1–7, and "no" to questions 8–10, you are probably on the right track. If you scored any differently, you may want to keep looking.

Maybe your child doesn't feel comfortable talking with your doctor, you're not confident the approach she's taking with your child will work, or perhaps the doctor wants your child to undergo an expensive test or treatment that isn't covered by your insurance.

Whatever your and your child's concerns may be, sometimes it pays to get a second opinion, especially when faced with a disorder that has many different treatment options, but no magic bullet. To find the names of ADHD specialists in your area, call your local branch of CHADD. You may also want to ask someone at your child's school for a recommendation, talk to other parents of children with ADHD for names of good specialists, or seek out good doctors from members of your ADHD support group.

It is important to be mindful that finding the right support can be frustrating for you and your child. Acknowledge the frustration and tell yourself that each step you take toward finding the right match for your family is a step in the right direction, even if each attempt may not seem initially successful. Reaching a "dead end" with a referral can be frustrating, but you are one step closer to finding the right support.

Important Points to Consider

The following is a list of important points to keep in mind during the diagnosis process:

1. Actively listen to and observe your child for signs and symptoms of ADHD.

2. Do not blame yourself for your child's ADHD symptoms. Understand that childhood ADHD is a neurological disorder.

3. When your child exhibits ADHD symptoms such as hyperactivity or inability to focus, remember to be calm and patient. Your goal is to understand your child's motivations, and yelling and screaming will not help achieve that goal.

4. Recognize that other parents may judge you, but do not allow their judgments to affect you or your relationship with your child. Your bond with your child is more important than anything else.

5. Know that an ADHD diagnosis can be confusing. Accept the confusion, but do not label it as "good" or "bad." Help your child cope with her confusion by starting a dialogue about how she is feeling on a day-to-day basis.

 **CHAPTER 3**

Understanding the Controversy Surrounding Preschool Children and ADHD

Infants and preschoolers may display some telltale signs of ADHD, but they are generally not diagnosed or treated for ADHD until they reach age six. Because preschoolers are by nature hyperactive, impulsive, and inattentive at times, it can be difficult to distinguish normal hyperactivity from that associated with ADHD. And although there are hundreds of scientific studies of how to diagnose ADHD in grade-school children, there are very few studies of how to detect the disorder in infants, toddlers, and preschool children. It is important to remember that your toddler or preschooler's hyperactivity does not mean he has ADHD. As a conscious parent, step back and try to see the whole picture, looking for patterns in behavior over time.

Can You Really Diagnose ADHD in Toddlers?

Most ADHD experts caution that it is very difficult to diagnose an infant or preschooler with ADHD. That's because many exhibit some ADHD symptoms in various situations that are actually developmentally appropriate for their age.

This is not to suggest that infants and preschoolers are never diagnosed with the condition. Some physicians believe it's prudent to diagnose the disorder in preschoolers and infants when impulsivity, hyperactivity, and inattention are extreme. For instance, a preschooler who can't focus on anything at all for any length of time and requires constant monitoring may be suspected of having ADHD by some diagnosticians.

> If your child is overly aggressive, exhibits behavior that is more extreme or very different than that of her peers, and has problems making friends, you may want to take her to a pediatrician or child psychologist for evaluation, especially if you or your spouse suffers from ADHD.

ADHD experts must look at the root of a child's behavior before making a definitive diagnosis, as many other things are often mistaken for ADHD, such as separation anxiety, poor motor skills or sensory problems, developmental disorders, oppositional disorder, and bipolar disorder.

Although most physicians will not diagnose an infant, toddler, or preschooler with ADHD, some believe there are certain behaviors in early childhood that can predict the onset of ADHD in later life. They include:

O Expulsion from preschool because of aggressive behavior

O Refusal to take part in school activities

O Unwillingness to respect other children's property and boundaries

O Being rejected, avoided, or shunned by peers

Again, these behaviors may not be enough to diagnose the condition in infants and toddlers, because they are naturally hyperactive.

Does My Toddler Have ADHD?

Although all toddlers have short attention spans and are only able to entertain themselves for a few minutes at a time, toddlers who may develop ADHD are often unable to sustain their attention even on their favorite toys or games for more than a few minutes, and are often distracted by the slightest sound or motion. They may also exhibit poor eye contact during conversation, and require far more one-on-one contact than other children to stay occupied and out of trouble.

> If your young child exhibits hyperactivity and problems focusing properly, you may find yourself in stressful situations quite often. Remember that instead of reacting to your child with anger, taking a step back, recognizing your emotion without judgment, and giving yourself time to come up with a peaceful solution can prevent further stress for both of you.

HYPER HYPERACTIVE

Although toddlers are also known for their high energy and activity levels and are naturally hyperactive, toddlers prone to ADHD are often in motion at all times. They are difficult to hold or cuddle and too hyperactive to eat or use the toilet. They are usually messy and careless and are constantly breaking or losing their toys. When these infants become excited, it can take hours to calm them down. With too much stimulation, they can exhibit wild behavior, such as hitting others and screaming at the top of their lungs.

OVERLY IMPULSIVE

Normal impulsiveness is also exaggerated in toddlers who go on to develop ADHD. They are likely to experience more falls and injuries, throw and break their toys more often, and experience trouble falling and staying asleep. A toddler who may develop ADHD is likely to wake up in the middle of the night with energy to burn and demand to play or run around. A lack of sleep is likely to make him more irritable and inattentive than other children.

Does My Preschooler Have ADHD?

Although children in this age group are usually still pretty inattentive, most children without ADHD are able to sit and do some activity on their own, such as listening to a story, coloring, or playing with toys.

By way of contrast, preschoolers who are likely to develop ADHD are usually unable to sit still and listen, play with toys on their own without problems, or concentrate on coloring for any length of time. A child without ADHD can do the same activity for ten to fifteen minutes, whereas a preschooler who may develop ADHD may need to change activities every few minutes.

Preschoolers who go on to develop ADHD may pick fights with their classmates, run out into the street without looking, fall out of trees, or get bitten by dogs they have pestered. They are usually in such a hurry that they can't sit still for a meal. Many preschoolers prone to the disorder will also become very talkative. If they have friends, the friends are likely to be very active children. Others may be expelled from school for hitting fellow classmates, destroying classroom materials, or displaying wild, uncontrollable behavior.

Research shows that many preschool children who go on to develop ADHD are very aggressive and have poor social skills. Studies show they are twice as disobedient as other children, are responsible for three times more stress in families, and misbehave five times as often as children without the disorder.

The Dangers of Early Diagnosis

One real danger of attempting to diagnose an infant, toddler, or pre-schooler with ADHD is that normal behavior is easy for teachers, parents, and even some ADHD experts to mistake for ADHD symptoms.

The *DSM-5* criteria used to diagnose ADHD point to red flags such as "out of seat during school," "does not follow through on instructions," "avoids tasks with sustained mental effort," and "fidgety and restless while sitting"—behavior that is demonstrated by nearly every toddler and pre-schooler. You know your child better than anyone else. Although it is important to be honest with yourself about your child's behavior, try not to judge your child as you do this. Simply recognize her behavior and do not give it a label of "good" or "bad." This portion of conscious parenting can help your child build strong confidence rather than worrying that her behavior is "inappropriate."

WASTED TIME AND EXPENSE

Another reason many experts are reluctant to diagnose ADHD in infants, toddlers, and preschoolers is that their bodies and brains are grow-ing and changing so quickly that isolating symptoms of ADHD can be difficult or impossible, especially because a diagnosis of ADHD rests on symptoms being present for at least six months in two different scenarios, such as at home, at school, and in social settings.

HOW DO YOU TREAT AN INFANT?

There's also the problem of how to treat an infant if she's been diagnosed with ADHD. Some experts claim that many parents can see signs of ADHD in children before they can even walk. They claim that infants who go on to develop ADHD often are squirmier, less able to cuddle, and have difficult temperaments. They may also be easily frustrated, impatient, and require more care and attention than other babies, and suffer from more colic.

Many physicians question how they can monitor infants and toddlers who are being treated for ADHD. Very few physicians would agree to give ADHD stimulant drugs to an infant who has been diagnosed with ADHD because they would have no way of knowing if the medication was working.

One study suggests that infant sleep patterns can predict ADHD in later years. The study examined infants with severe or chronic sleep problems and then looked at them again when the children were five and a half years old. One in four of the infants had developed ADHD compared to one in twenty children in the general population who had developed ADHD.

Pros and Cons of a "Wait and See" Approach

Studies show that young children diagnosed with the condition between the ages of two and four have a 50 percent chance of outgrowing it, whereas children diagnosed after age five have only a 25 percent chance. Considering the odds, some experts believe that when it comes to diagnosing ADHD, the younger the better.

On the other hand, diagnosing an infant or preschooler with a disorder that isn't normally diagnosed until age six opens a Pandora's box. You and your child could go through a lot of expense and heartache for nothing. There's also the chance that diagnosing an infant or toddler with what appears to be ADHD will distract you or your physician from recognizing telltale signs of disorders that mimic ADHD, or have similar symptoms, and which are far more common in infants and toddlers.

Remember that it is important to be patient with your child and yourself when seeking a diagnosis for ADHD. Your child doesn't want to be stuck sitting in a waiting room any more than you do, so be prepared by giving yourself some time before each doctor's visit to do some deep breathing and calming exercises, and ask your child to participate as well.

The Preschool ADHD Treatment Study (PATS)

Another problem in diagnosing infants, toddlers, and preschoolers with ADHD is how to effectively treat symptoms. PATS, a study conducted by the National Institute of Mental Health (NIMH) in 2006, was the first long-term study designed to look at the effectiveness of treating preschoolers with ADHD with behavior therapy and/or methylphenidate. The study looked at 300 preschoolers with severe ADHD who had histories of preschool expulsion and rejection by peers.

PARENT TRAINING

In the first stage of the study, the preschoolers and their parents took part in a ten-week behavior therapy course. Parents were trained in behavior modification techniques, including giving consistent praise, ignoring negative behavior, and using time-outs. More than a third of the children responded so favorably to behavior modification that they did not go on to the medication phase of the study.

MEDICATING PRESCHOOLERS

Children with extreme ADHD symptoms who did not improve with behavior therapy participated in a double-blind study comparing low doses of methylphenidate (Ritalin) with a placebo. Methylphenidate treatment resulted in a significant reduction in ADHD symptoms, as measured by standard rating forms and observations at home and at school.

However, the study reported that the children's ability to tolerate the drugs was less than expected. Eleven percent of the children ultimately stopped treatment, despite improvements in ADHD symptoms, because of moderate to severe side effects. These included a reduction in appetite, an increase in insomnia and anxiety, emotional outbursts, repetitive behaviors and thoughts, and irritability. Preschoolers appeared to be more susceptible to side effects than children in elementary school.

One adverse effect of stimulant medication is that it appears to slow the growth rate of preschoolers. Children who participated in the PATS study and took stimulant drugs grew a half-inch less and weighed three pounds less than normal growth rates.

THE MEDICATION CONTROVERSY

Experts remain divided on whether preschool children should take drugs to control ADHD symptoms. Some feel that the methodology for diagnosing infants and toddlers is unreliable, as are the effects of drugs on a developing brain, and that more research is needed before infants, toddlers, and preschoolers are given medication for ADHD. Others argue that because the PATS study showed that some young children with ADHD benefited from ADHD medication, those with severe ADHD should be treated to control out-of-control behavior.

The Controversy Regarding TV and ADHD

Research has also shown a connection between attention deficit problems and watching excessive amounts of television. According to the guidelines of the American Academy of Pediatrics (AAP), children younger than two years old should not watch TV, DVDs, computers, video games, videotapes, or other types of entertainment on screens. Children two years and older should be limited to about two hours daily of "quality" TV programs, such as educational television programs.

Remember to balance TV watching with in-the-moment, quality time with your child. Talk to her as much as possible and listen to what she has to say. This will help build strong emotional connections for years to come.

However, many ADHD experts disagree that television is a menace for children with ADHD, and are not overly concerned if young children watch a limited amount of educational television and innocent shows containing characters such as Winnie the Pooh or Thomas the Tank Engine. Children with ADHD as well as those without it enjoy watching favorite videos over and over again, and often pick up new words and concepts from them that they wouldn't otherwise learn until much later.

Pro-television ADHD experts argue that children who don't watch any television at all are likely to be out of the cultural mainstream, and appear "out of it" to classmates and teachers because they can't share in the excitement of television shows and sports events.

Be aware that "screen time" can be misused by parents as a way to get through a meal or keep your child entertained or quiet during wait times. A short educational iPad game or a video of *Sesame Street* may not be harmful in and of itself, but make sure you aren't using it to placate your child when he is fussy or impatient. Doing so will only teach him that he gets rewarded with screen time if he throws a fit. Avoid using screens during wait times and at meals, as you will be depriving your child of learning how to wait appropriately without screen entertainment.

Survival Tips for Parents

If your infant or preschooler is exhibiting symptoms that you think may signal ADHD, don't panic or jump to conclusions. Your child may be acting normally for his age.

If your child demonstrates extreme behavior that is much different from other children his age, or if he has difficulty making friends, you may want to take him to a pediatrician or child psychologist for a comprehensive medical and developmental history that includes feedback from teachers and health professionals who have worked with your child.

Neuropsychological testing may also be required to rule out conditions that mimic or overlap with ADHD, including anxiety disorder, language-processing disorders, oppositional defiant disorder, and sensory integration problems.

BEHAVIOR TREATMENT FOR PRESCHOOL CHILDREN

Behavior treatment for preschool children with ADHD involves adjusting their environment to help them with social interactions. As a parent, you can help your child overcome challenges by creating more structure, clearly stating expectations, limiting choices to avoid overstimulation, being consistent when it comes to disciplining your child, setting rewards and consequences, and creating routines that help your child get and stay organized. For more on behavior modification, see Chapter 14.

An excellent way to bolster the confidence and self-esteem of your child with ADHD is to help him discover his special gifts and talents, then provide him with the instruction, resources, teachers, mentors, and materials he needs to excel in that gift or talent. Many children with ADHD are extremely creative and intuitive, so look for ways to help your child shine.

PARENT TRAINING

Because children with ADHD don't come with an owner's manual and require special care and discipline, you may also benefit from parent training, which can teach you helpful strategies for disciplining your child and tips for getting and keeping him organized.

You may also want to join a support group of parents of children with ADHD to gain insight on the disorder and how to handle it, as well as information on local resources, such as the best physicians and ADHD practitioners. Your local area may also have mindful parenting classes available. These classes may not be targeted toward parents of children with ADHD specifically, but the tools and support will likely be helpful to both you and your child nonetheless.

THE BOTTOM LINE

Remember that children with ADHD have problems controlling their behavior without treatment or medication and may be as baffled by their symptoms as you are. Don't mistake ADHD symptoms for intentional misbehaving.

In preparing your child for preschool or daycare, work with teachers and personnel to create an effective learning environment for your child that has lots of built-in structure and routine that substitutes for the chronic disorganization that typically accompanies childhood ADHD.

Be honest about your child's limitations as well as his special gifts so teachers can make modifications that can help your child with ADHD thrive. Understand that even with the best of treatment, your child may still be more hyperactive and impulsive than normal children and may require special classes and accommodations.

MINDFULNESS ACTIVITIES FOR YOUR PRESCHOOLER

The image of a very young child engaging in mindfulness may conjure up an image of trying to make a wiggly worm sit still. It is true that getting toddlers and preschoolers to sit for extended periods of time, especially when they are prone to hyperactivity, may seem impossible. It is not very realistic to try to get her to meditate on her own. However, it is totally appropriate to share your meditation with her: Simply hold your child in your lap while you practice your meditation. She may be comforted by the stillness and by the presence of your body.

Another way to start to encourage mindfulness in your young child is to practice a few age-appropriate activities such as:

○ Bring your child's attention to her senses. Point out the sounds and sights you hear on a walk and encourage her to describe her surroundings. Making this into a game (e.g. using your "Spidey senses" for Spider-Man fans) can make the experience enjoyable for your child.

○ Teach deep breathing by having your child "rock" a favorite stuffed animal to sleep. Have your child lie down and put a stuffed animal on his belly. Then, using his breath, see if he can "rock the stuffed animal to sleep" by moving it up and down with deep breathing. This activity is particularly good for trying to get your child to wind down at night.

O Blowing bubbles is another fun way to encourage deep breathing in a young child.

O Model for your young child "mindful tasting" by describing the texture, smell, and taste of what you are eating and asking him to do the same.

O Reading to your child can be a relaxing and singular focus activity. For children with particularly short attention spans, you might use books that have a sensory aspect to them, such as touching different textures or turning "peek-a-book" flaps.

Important Points to Consider

Keeping your cool in stressful situations can be difficult, especially when your toddler or preschooler exhibits hyperactive tendencies. Here is a list of things to help you keep calm and positive:

1. Just because your toddler or preschooler gets excited every once in a while or has trouble focusing from time to time does not mean she has ADHD. Remember to keep perspective and look at your child's behavior as a whole.

2. Although your major goal as a conscious parent is to stay connected and present with your child as much as possible, allowing your child to watch some TV can help her learn social cues and build her vocabulary.

3. There are many mindful activities you can try with your child to help calm her down if she seems hyperactive.

4. Be honest with your child's teachers and caregivers about his behavior. Keeping an open line of communication will be beneficial for everyone, including your child.

 **CHAPTER 4**

ADHD in Grade School Children

Children with ADHD struggle in traditional classrooms and are commonly viewed by their teachers as underachievers. Many come to think of themselves as not very bright or unmotivated. The real problem is that their minds work differently from most people's. They are more holistic in their thinking and are drawn to abstract ideas rather than details. Because they focus on the "wrong" parts of the lessons, they can easily forget, mix up, or simply overlook information that teachers consider important. One of the best ways to give your child confidence is to praise her skills and unique capabilities as much as possible. Remind her to be kind to herself, and to find value in her abilities. Also remind her to communicate with her teacher as much as possible, especially if she is having trouble understanding something in class.

The Best Types of Classrooms
for Children with ADHD

ADHD experts agree that the best classroom for grade school children with ADHD is an informal one—that is, not the type of class where children are expected to sit in the same seat all day long. They are better off in a classroom where they can move around, stand up, or work at their own pace.

Your child's classroom should be sufficiently structured so that it provides your child with a framework and lots of cues and tools that help her get and stay organized, such as calendars, schedules, assignments posted prominently and in the same place; designated work spaces for learning tools such as workbooks, textbooks, technology, etc.; and well-organized supplies.

Students with ADHD also thrive in a classroom setting where the schedule is structured and orderly, with the sequence of classes consistent from one day to the next, and special classes, such as art or music, held on the same days every week.

ORGANIZING THE SCHOOL YEAR OR SEMESTER

Children with ADHD often have challenges getting and staying organized and planning ahead. They also tend to have midseason slumps after the novelty of the first few months of school wears off and the end of school is still months away.

To help your child maintain her focus, work with the child's teacher to create a list of academic goals and milestones your child can work toward, and have her cross off each one as she completes it.

Review the list with your child every week to see how things are progressing, to see if deadlines are being met, and to look at what remains to be completed. Remember that setting up lots of external cues for your child can help compensate for her internal lack of organization.

STRUCTURING ASSIGNMENTS AND HOMEWORK

Many children with ADHD have difficulty completing large, many-step projects with deadlines. Because they are poor at organizing, prioritizing, and handling details, they often become so overwhelmed they give up in midstream and never finish the project.

To help your child stay on track and finish projects on time, encourage her teacher to break up large projects into doable mini-projects, and to give each mini-project a deadline so your child doesn't get behind.

It will also help if her teacher gives your child one instruction at a time, rather than several lumped together. Instead of telling your child to put away her math paper, get out her English grammar book, and turn in her science homework, have the teacher give her one instruction at a time.

SPECIAL SERVICES

If your child has not yet been diagnosed with ADHD, but you think he may have it or a teacher has concerns, one option is to ask that the school conduct an evaluation to determine if your child qualifies for special accommodations or education services. See Chapter 9 for more information about getting the appropriate support for your child.

Performance Problems Associated with ADHD

Many students diagnosed with ADHD do well in school one year and flounder the next. That should make it obvious that the classroom environment, teaching method, and a goodness of fit are important for children with ADHD.

EASILY BORED

Many children with ADHD are very independent from the time they are young, and this characteristic is especially common among the intellectually gifted. Individualists often clash with their teachers even if they are not disruptive. Some read books in class instead of doing busy-work assignments. Some draw instead of sitting with their hands folded on their desks. Some create complex stories in their imaginations to fend off boredom. They persist because what they are doing interests them. Parents' and teachers' negative opinions are less compelling to children with ADHD than their desire to stimulate and express themselves.

PROBLEMS WITH DETAILS

Many children with ADHD also have a holistic thinking style that focuses on the big picture at the expense of details that they find boring or mind-numbing. They have problems automatically focusing on elements that define subtle differences, which are required to sort and organize.

Many kids with ADHD are adept at comprehending complex concepts and developing new ones, but they are abysmal at performing simple computations that require rote memorization.

HYPERFOCUS

At the same time, kids with ADHD often hyperfocus on subjects and ideas they find interesting, to the exclusion of everything else. For instance, it's not uncommon for a child with ADHD to spend hours on a subject or idea she enjoys, while ignoring her math or grammar homework that's due the next day.

The ability to concentrate intensely can be an asset—especially when a child with ADHD goes to college, where creativity and thinking outside the box are more highly valued. Unfortunately, in grade school, a child's hyperfocus often gets in the way of learning or completing nuts-and-bolts ("boring") ideas and assignments that lay the groundwork for grander ideas.

Understanding Behavior Associated with ADHD

Many children with ADHD have short fuses and are easily overwhelmed, frustrated, and discouraged. In addition, they may suffer from oppositional defiant disorder, or behavior characterized by disobedience, hostility, and defiance toward authority figures, including teachers. This makes it more difficult for them to get along with people, take directions, and get things done.

UNDERSTANDING HYPERACTIVITY

Many children with ADHD are hyperactive, which can make it difficult for them to pay attention, focus, or even stay in their seats. Hyperactive children often need a constructive way to combat boredom and release excess energy. If your child is restless or frustrated, do not nag or suggest a sedentary activity, such as television or reading. As a conscious parent, the best thing to do is recommend somersaults, jump rope, hitting a tennis ball against the side of the house, or going for a walk. Try doing these activities along with your child if you can. At least suggest that your child stand up and stretch for a few moments. Also, consider using a standing desk at home for your child to do homework, so she can move while she works.

THE ROLE OF EXERCISE

Another way to ease your child's hyperactivity is to ensure he gets plenty of exercise. For many students, gym is their only chance to move about, but many schools have cut back so that students only attend a few times a week. Even if they go every day, they average only nine minutes of exercise per class. The rest of the time is spent watching others or listening to the teacher.

A study by United States International University and reported in Thomas Armstrong's *The Myth of the A.D.D. Child* found that exercise has positive effects on behavior. Hyperactive, aggressive students participating in jumping or field exercises forty minutes a day, three times a week were less aggressive on the days they ran than on the days they did not.

Exercising for twenty minutes prior to homework time can have an added benefit of increased focus. Sometimes students who have been made to sit all day at school need some sort of activity prior to sitting down to do their homework. You might also infuse a mindfulness ritual right before homework time, such as selecting a mantra ("focus," "get it done and then have more fun") that your child can say to himself during a few minutes of deep breathing.

REGARDED AS ODD AND DIFFERENT

Highly creative children are in the minority, and the majority does not understand how they think or why they behave as they do. Peers tend to regard them as strange or odd because of their unusual interests. Especially creative types are often branded as crazy because their heightened sensitivity causes them to have stronger emotional reactions than less sensitive people. Even if creative teens find a social niche in high school, they know that most of their peers regard them as odd.

Others label themselves as "crazy" and withdraw. Some hold everyone at a distance for fear of having their "insanity" discovered. Some embrace the role and spend years moving through the revolving door of the mental health system. When creative children are not accepted by their peers, affirmation from parents becomes all the more important. Most parents love their children dearly. But too many make creative youngsters feel that something is terribly wrong with them. Remind your child that she is unique, and that there is nothing "wrong" with her. When teaching your child to be mindful, you can also remind her to try and avoid labeling herself and/or her behavior as "good" or "bad."

DAYDREAMING

In addition, some children with ADHD are accused of being lazy because they daydream. Often the real "problem" is that they devote a lot of mental energy to pondering the material being presented rather than simply trying to commit it to memory. They consider its relationship to other things they have learned and contemplate its implications.

Highly sensitive children react strongly to sounds, temperature changes, smells, and tastes that others barely notice. Such acute sensitivity often goes hand in hand with artistic, musical, and literary genius. Do not assume your child is exaggerating when he complains about discomforts that to you seem minor.

OUTSPOKEN AND SPEAKING AS EQUALS

Some children with ADHD also tend to be outspoken. They are prone to address adults as equals rather than deferring to their authority. If they are generally insensitive to other people's feelings, they may alienate peers and earn a reputation among adults for being ill-mannered.

Maintaining good relationships with teachers and classmates can be especially challenging for independent types who love to debate. Some children consider ideas more important than people's feelings.

Help your child understand how his behavior affects others, but let him decide whether he wants to change in order to be liked. It is a mistake to take your youngster's side against teachers, but it is also a mistake to try to change your child into someone he is not. A better approach is to communicate in no uncertain terms that you expect your child to be respectful of others. Discuss ways he can assert himself appropriately. And when he hurts someone's feelings, he of course needs to apologize.

DIFFICULTY BEING ON TIME AND ADHERING TO SCHEDULES

Children with ADHD frequently have problems sticking to schedules, in part because dividing time into slots and assigning activities to each one does not strike them as sensible. If they worry about being late, it may be because they are afraid others will be upset. They do not believe that the passage of time is significant or that the clock should rule people's lives.

Help Build Structure and Organization

Poor organizational skills are one of the hallmark signals of childhood ADHD and kids may have difficulty organizing everything from items and activities to school tasks. For your grade school child, this may manifest as having problems getting homework and assignments done on time or in an organized fashion, being unable to find clothing or toys, and living amidst constant clutter.

The first step toward helping your child get organized is to help her overcome her natural aversion to it. The second step is finding ways to help your child get and stay organized. The third and most important is having the entire family commit to using the strategies to help keep the family member with ADHD on track.

OVERCOMING AVERSION

Until your child understands the benefit of getting and staying organized, she will probably resist it. After all, organizing can be tedious, repetitive, and boring—things that children with ADHD already have a natural aversion to. However, most children with ADHD can be motivated to accomplish something. Incentives, such as a raise in her weekly allowance or a special gift, may help motivate your child.

How can you help your child become more organized and enjoy doing it? The best way to help your child succeed is to make organizing fun by making her feel like a team member rather than a victim, and by keeping an upright and enthusiastic attitude. Look on *www.pinterest.com* together for fun organizational ideas and have her be an active participant in picking ones that she likes.

Ask your child what areas or activities she wants to organize better. Discuss some of the problems she can avoid by getting more organized, and the many benefits she'll enjoy—such as having more time to play because she's not spending all her time searching for her shoes. Keep track of how your child's disorganization sabotages her school grades and friendships, and discuss this with your child so she better understands the ramifications of being disorganized in her own life.

CLEAN YOUR ROOM!

Few things spark more arguments between children and parents than messy rooms. If your child can't find anything in her room, be realistic about what she can accomplish. Your child may not be able to maintain a room that's neat as a pin, but it shouldn't be total chaos either.

These simple tips can help your child to declutter:

○ Give every item in your child's room a designated "home" so she knows where it belongs.

○ Create a daily five-minute routine in which your child puts things away and returns them to their home locations. Then reward her.

○ Every two months, help your child donate toys and clothing she no longer uses or wants to a charity; store items she only occasionally uses on shelves or in storage elsewhere.

○ Be persistent and provide lots of friendly reminders and supervision, but let your child do the work herself.

○ Find a way to make organizing and tidying up enjoyable and fun. Maintain a supportive, enthusiastic attitude, be realistic about what your child can actually accomplish and maintain, and provide clear, consistent requests. Your child won't do anything if she gets discouraged, overwhelmed, or frustrated.

Develop Routines

All children, and especially children with ADHD, thrive on routine, even if they claim they hate it. According to a review of fifty years of psychological research published in the *Journal of Family Psychology*, even infants and preschoolers enjoy better health and behavior when the family has consistent and predicable routines.

Routines are essential for a child or teen with ADHD if he is to focus on daily tasks and activities without getting frustrated or flustered because of ADHD symptoms of inattention, lack of focus, the tendency to get distracted and restless, and low or zero tolerance for boring, repetitive activities.

MORNING ROUTINE

To help your child get to school on time, try these simple strategies:

- Have your child wake up at the same time every morning, and go straight to the bathroom. If he has trouble waking up, set an alarm.

- Put out clothing the night before so your child doesn't have to worry about finding clothing to wear in the morning.

- Set out a healthy breakfast while he's getting dressed, and have him eat it without the distraction of TVs, phones, computers, or toys.

- Have his coat and school bag by the door waiting for him.

- Have a set time for your child to walk out the door.

THE HOMEWORK ROUTINE

Most children with ADHD need a mental breather after school, so give your child about thirty minutes to unwind by playing, watching TV or video games, exercising, or eating a snack. After that time is over use the following routine:

- Create a regular place and time for your child to do his homework.

- To help your child transition from relaxing to doing homework, give him a ten-minute warning.

- Help your child review his homework assignment, and make sure he has pencils and other supplies handy.

- Build in short breaks so your child can get up and walk around and stretch for a few minutes to decrease restlessness and clear his mind.

- Be generous with praise, applauding your child's efforts as well as his results.

- Sit down with him and go over his completed homework.

- Organize assignments and school supplies needed for the next day, put them in his school bag, and set it by the front door.

- Do something relaxing and enjoyable together after your child completes his homework.

THE SUPPER ROUTINE

If possible, eat dinner together as a family at a regularly scheduled time every night. Establish a few dinnertime routines for your child, such as helping prepare the meal, setting the table, clearing the table, or putting the dishes in the dishwasher. Don't discuss work, school, or family problems or issues around the dinner table. Keep the conversation light and friendly, and don't eat with the TV on or phones at the table. Practice mindful eating together as a family for at least a portion of your meal, in which you focus on the sensory experience of eating and enjoy each other's company.

BEDTIME ROUTINE

Establish a regular bedtime routine on school nights so your child gets to sleep on time and gets the sleep he needs.

O Give him a five- or ten-minute warning before it's time to start his bedtime routine.

O Have your child turn off the TV or computer or put away his toys.

O Help your child select and lay out his clothing for the next day.

O Have your child bathe, brush his teeth, put on his pajamas, and get into bed.

O Read a story together or have a friendly talk to help your child unwind.

O Kiss your child good night, turn off the lights, and wish him pleasant dreams.

Your child may respond to visual cues of routines, such as smartphone pictures of himself in each of the steps and in the final step. For example, you can show the picture of what it looks like to be "ready for bed" so he can start to visualize and internalize the steps it takes to get there.

Helping Your Child Overcome Frustrations, Setbacks, and Competition

It's important to understand the developmental level of your child before she goes to school. She may be able to perform at grade level academically, but be several years behind her peers in terms of maturity and social skills.

If this is the case, it's important that you keep your expectations realistic, and not expect your child to behave as maturely as other children her age. In fact, it may help to simply consider her two or three years younger than she really is.

SOLUTIONS AT SCHOOL

As a parent, you should also work with your child's teacher to help her develop simple strategies that will make things easier for your child in a classroom setting. Remember to be calm and speak lovingly to your child.

- Make sure the teacher understands that it's crucial never to humiliate or embarrass your child when she engages in inappropriate behavior. Many children with ADHD don't learn social skills by osmosis like other children, but must be taught them by teachers and parents.

- Ask your child's teacher to work privately with your child to practice appropriate responses to peers.

- Request that the teacher provide lots of chances for your child to work in small groups with patient peers where she can practice her social skills.

- Ask the teacher to monitor your child's interactions with classmates to help minimize problems.

- Talk to your child's teacher about praising her in front of classmates when she does a good job on something. This will help heighten your child's confidence and self-esteem and is a more constructive way to let other students know about your child's special gifts and aptitudes than having your child showing off or resorting to rude comments to get attention.

○ Make sure the teacher understands that your child should not be compared to other children in the class, especially if your child has been mainstreamed. Most children with ADHD are not lazy or unmotivated, but are trying as hard as they can to succeed despite their ADHD shortcomings. Many children with ADHD who are forced to compete against others become so anxious their symptoms flare.

MINDFULNESS ACTIVITIES FOR YOUR GRADE-SCHOOL-AGE CHILD

Grade-school-age children are ideal candidates for learning mindfulness techniques, because they often have greater control than young children and they haven't developed a resistance to parents' ideas, as a teenager might. Here are a few activities you can do with your child to practice mindfulness:

○ Pick a morning activity that you can be mindful of, such as brushing your teeth, eating breakfast, or taking a shower. Encourage your child to think about the sensory aspects of the activity (what he hears, feels, smells, or tastes).

○ Set aside two to five minutes a day for a deep breathing activity. Make it fun by using imagery (e.g. imagine you are blowing out candles on a birthday cake with each breath).

○ Teach a yoga pose each week and practice focusing on the breath as you and your child hold the pose for a minute or two.

○ Have your child pretend she is a statue and see how long she can practice standing still. Use a "magic wand" to unfreeze her after thirty seconds. Then try to increase the intervals.

○ Play a game in which your child has to use her senses to identify an object. Have a "mystery bag" filled with objects and let her pick one. Without looking, have her feel the object, describe its shape, texture, and size, and then guess what the object is.

○ At snack time, practice mindful eating by playing "guess the snack." Have your child close her eyes, touch the snack, smell the snack, and then eat the snack. Have her describe what she sees, smells, and tastes.

○ During homework, have your child pick a mantra to keep her on track (e.g. "keep going," "stay focused," "other things can wait").

○ At nighttime, have a mindfulness bedtime ritual, such as progressive muscle relaxation (e.g. tensing and releasing muscles one by one) or a guided imagery recording.

Important Points to Consider

Staying conscious and in the moment can take practice and time, but the more you work at it, the easier it becomes. Sooner or later, it will become second nature. Try reminding yourself of these key points as you progress:

1. Praise your child as much as possible. Over time, your praise will help her build confidence in her skills and abilities. Be sure to use specific praise (e.g. I like how you remembered your permission slip) instead of general praise (e.g. good job) so she knows what she is doing well.

2. Creating a routine can help curb stress at bedtime and in the morning. This allows you to spend more enjoyable quality time with your child, helping to build positive emotional bonds.

3. Teach your children yoga and stretches to help them remove excess energy. Doing these exercises with them is even better. Yoga increases focus, relaxation, mind-body balance, and inner harmony.

4. When it comes to homework, help your child through difficult tasks and offer gentle encouragement instead of nagging her to finish her assignments.

5. Although organization may come to you naturally, for a child with ADHD, it can be difficult. Help your child appreciate the benefits of staying organized, but don't organize for her. Offer support instead.

6. Help your child understand social cues by explaining behavior to her, instead of getting angry if she doesn't understand it herself without your help. Take a step back and remind yourself that patience is key.

 **CHAPTER 5**

ADHD in Middle School Adolescents

Entering middle school is a huge leap forward for any child, but for a preteen with ADHD, the leap is longer, higher, and harder. Instead of staying in the same class all day with one teacher, your tween moves from classroom to classroom, interacting with different teachers and students and carrying everything he needs with him. Many teens with ADHD lack the organizational skills needed to keep track of schedules, homework, and supplies. The desire to fit in can make the middle school years even more challenging for tweens with ADHD who lack confidence and social skills. As a conscious parent, it is important to give your child support as he navigates these difficult waters. When your child faces a difficult situation, encourage him to remain calm and focused so he can approach the issue with a clear mind.

A Difficult Transition

The many new social and academic demands of middle school aren't easy for a tween with ADHD. To make it worse, research shows that ADHD symptoms often worsen as a child enters his tween years.

Even if your child excelled in grade school, he may struggle with staying organized as he moves from one classroom to another and works with a variety of new and different teachers who have high expectations. Coping with peer pressure, teasing, bullying, and the pressure cooker of adolescent dating and social life and hormonal changes may exacerbate his social awkwardness and tax his fragile social skills to the breaking point, thereby causing him to feel increasingly insecure, self-conscious, and like a social outcast.

As any parent can attest, any tween going through puberty experiences a variety of growing pains. For a child struggling with ADHD, the transition from childhood to adulthood is likely to be even rockier. What's a parent to do?

Contrary to popular myth, ADHD is not just a condition that affects children. Nearly 80 percent of children with ADHD go on to have symptoms as adolescents, teenagers, and adults, according to the National Institute of Mental Health. Adolescents and teens with ADHD are likely to view the world as an overwhelming whirlwind of confusing activity that requires a host of skills they struggle with.

Tweens with ADHD are easily distracted, which means they often lose track of time. Getting to class on time several times a day, as one must do in middle school, can be particularly difficult for your child. Make sure your child's teachers and principal know he has the disorder, and encourage your child to be honest with his teachers if difficulties arise.

What might come easily or naturally to other tweens may be an enormous, exhausting task for your tween, including such necessary skills as planning ahead, completing projects, staying on track, prioritizing projects, breaking down large projects into small, doable pieces, organizing schoolwork, homework, and activities, following conversations, making new friends, and adapting to a continual onslaught of new teachers and students.

Dealing with ADHD-Related Academic Challenges

The middle school years are the years when students integrate and build on the three Rs they learned in grade school. They also develop the cognitive skills needed for more complex thinking and reasoning, such as being able to think in abstract terms, deduce and interpret material, and understand ambiguity.

Unfortunately, many tweens with ADHD are two to three years behind other tweens developmentally, and may lack the brain wiring to develop cognitive skills required for more independent learning and self-regulation, such as planning, organizing, and using study skills strategies effectively. While many kids with ADHD are often strong in abstract, creative, and holistic thinking, they may lack the attention to detail and independent-learning skills to complete work, and do so efficiently, without adult guidance.

HOW YOUR CHILD'S TEACHER CAN HELP

If your child is not eligible for special accommodations and services, consider working with her teacher to develop strategies that will help your child better cope with ADHD learning challenges.

O Help your child build better study skills. Many tweens with ADHD have poor recall, and may have problems storing and retrieving subject matter they recently read. Your teacher can help your child by showing her how to isolate material in her textbooks that's most likely to appear on tests by paying attention to boxes, colored fonts, sidebars, and chapter summaries.

O Use who, what, where, when, and how as cues for learning. If your child is studying history, she can ask: who are the main characters, what is going on, where is it occurring, when did it happen, and how did it happen to help her remember important facts.

O Find tricks to master math. Succeeding at math requires following a succession of steps to solve a problem. Creating sample problems and math formulas on note cards and keeping them in one place will provide a handy and helpful reminder for your child.

O Improve your child's reading awareness. Effective reading requires your child to be able to skim and scan to find important facts, and read critically. Many children with ADHD have problems with all of these skills because they lose focus when scanning, and have trouble understanding ideas that are presented or restated in a different way. Highlighting important information can help your child keep track of facts. Summarizing and elaborating on the major points in the story can also help increase comprehension.

O Find ways for your child to overcome ADHD restlessness. Many tweens with ADHD are restless and may require periodic breaks to maintain focus and concentration. Encourage the teacher to find an unobtrusive way to let your child take physical breaks so she can refocus.

HOW YOU AS A PARENT CAN HELP

Your middle school child will likely benefit from the same type of structure and guidance you provided when he was younger, even if he is more resistant to it as a middle schooler. When helping your child to traverse his rocky middle school years, remember that nagging him most likely won't produce success. Try being supportive and quietly nonjudgmental. Here are seven other suggestions to try:

1. Send your middle school child off to school with a "success pack" for each teacher that includes a letter signed by you (and your spouse or partner, if you have one) that introduces your child, describes her medical condition, hobbies, and goals, and explains that ADHD is not an excuse for poor academic performance or behavior. This makes the teacher aware of your child's condition, and provides details about how to contact you if problems arise.

2. Develop a contract with your child for school-related performance and behavior that needs improvement, and provide incentives for success, such as an increase in her allowance.

3. Find the best teachers for your child. Ask the principal to switch your child into classes taught by teachers who have experience with ADHD, or rearrange your child's schedule so the most challenging classes fall at a time of day when she's likely to be most alert and attentive.

4. Be on the lookout for learning disabilities in your child. Many learning disabilities don't surface until middle school, especially in very bright children. Telltale symptoms might include a reluctance to read or write, an inability to comprehend what she reads, difficulty understanding abstract concepts, and poor writing and handwriting skills. If you suspect your child has a learning disorder, consult with your school psychologist or resource specialist teacher about your concerns. You may request that your school formally evaluate your child if general education supports are not working.

5. Children and tweens with ADHD have notoriously sloppy handwriting because of ADHD-related problems with fine motor skill coordination. Ask your child's teacher if your tween can use a computer to take notes and complete homework assignments, reports, and essay tests, instead of doing them longhand.

6. Network and visit the school to ensure the teachers and administrators know you. Your child will benefit if you get involved at school, and know who to go to when problems crop up. Go to school board meetings, and volunteer to help in the classroom.

7. Create iron-clad structures and routines at home. Beginning and completing tasks are difficult for children with ADHD. Routines are a good way to help children learn cognitive skills they need at school for organizing, starting and finishing work, and planning. Whether it's getting to bed on time or catching the school bus, create easy, set routines for your child to follow.

Helping Your Tween Get and Stay Organized

Staying organized can be a nightmare for your child when he reaches middle school and suddenly has multiple classes and teachers. Skills that other students might learn naturally or take for granted—filing papers, remembering what books, binders, and implements are needed for each class, completing homework, and creating notebooks for each subject—don't come naturally to kids with ADHD; they must be taught.

As mentioned earlier, as a conscious parent, one of your major goals is to be supportive without nagging. This can take practice. If you find yourself beginning to nag your child, take a step back and realign your approach.

Middle school work is inherently more complex than grade school work and demands a higher level of cognitive functioning—such as classifying information, assembling facts, and following a certain progression of steps. If your child already struggles with focus and memory, it's essential that you and your child's teacher establish structures for your child that will help keep him on track.

HOW YOUR CHILD'S TEACHERS CAN HELP

Schedule a meeting with your child's teachers before the start of school, and ask if they can implement some of the following learning tools when teaching your child:

O Post and hand out personal copies of schedules, checklists, study guides, and class notes, or make them available electronically so you can help your child stay on track.

O Provide lots of advance warning about upcoming projects and reports. Give students with ADHD a head start by helping them select a topic, making sure they have the materials they need, and reviewing outlines and rough drafts.

○ Break up big projects into bite-sized pieces and establish periodic checkpoints so students with ADHD can monitor their progress and stay on track. Post deadlines prominently, and make sure students with ADHD copy them in their notebooks. Refer to deadlines frequently. Contact parents to ensure they know about projects and when they are due.

HOW PARENTS CAN HELP

The teacher is only part of the success equation. As the parent of a child with ADHD, it's up to you to make sure your child does his homework on time.

To ensure your child brings home homework assignments, suggest he have a homework buddy he can contact in the event he forgets. If your child has problems copying homework assignments into his notebook, ask the school if he can take a photo of the assignment with his phone, or dictate it into the voice memo function on his phone. Some teachers and schools also have websites that post homework due. Teach your child to check these websites every day, regardless of whether or not he thinks something is due.

Teach your child how to make good "to-do" lists, dividing tasks into "now" and "later." Review his list every evening for the next day, and remind him about projects and assignments that are due the next day.

Before school starts, help your child set up a notebook that's divided into sections, or get him a different color notebook for each subject.

And don't forget to give your child lots of feedback and praise for a job well done. Kids with ADHD get so much criticism they become adept at tuning it out. Using praise is far more effective.

Teaching Your Child Time-Management Skills

Prioritizing is a basic time-management skill. A good time to help your child learn is when helping her decide on the order for doing homework assignments. Some students prefer to do the easiest ones first, because it boosts their confidence. Others prefer to tackle the harder items first when they are fresher, and they can relax once those are finished. Or use "chaining," a behavior therapy technique that lets your child do the task she likes least first, then reward herself for finishing that task by doing something she enjoys next. This practice motivates your child to get through the first assignment.

Children diagnosed with ADHD tend to be remarkably unaware of the passage of time. As a consequence, they commonly misjudge how much time is required to complete routine tasks. For example, they underestimate how long it will take them to get ready to go somewhere or do a chore, and they exaggerate the amount of time they spend on activities they dislike.

Help your child list tasks and put them in order before she sets out to do any project that has given her difficulty in the past. Consider making and posting lists in convenient locations to guide her through washing the dishes, straightening her room, and packing her bookbag. Children with poor memories for such details should use as many aids as possible. After referring to their lists and checking off each completed task and step over a period of weeks, months, or years, they will undoubtedly memorize the procedure.

To learn to cope with deadlines, youngsters need to be able to judge how much time various projects will take and set up schedules matched to their capabilities and, whenever possible, their desires.

The first step is to collect lots of data about how long it takes them to do all kinds of routine tasks: taking a bath, completing a set of math problems, gathering their things together for baseball practice, walking home from a friend's house, and so on. That information will eventually enable them to make realistic estimates about how much time they need to allow themselves for various tasks.

Importance and Challenges of Peer Approval

Middle school children feel more socially vulnerable than practically any other age group. For children with ADHD, who can be socially awkward, the challenges are even greater to fit in, handle peer pressure, and feel comfortable in a variety of new social gatherings and settings.

Even for children without ADHD, the rules for being accepted can seem so arbitrary and changeable that kids are kept constantly on their toes. For kids with ADHD, who often lack social confidence and have trouble reading nonverbal cues and body language, committing a middle school social faux pas is practically inevitable.

Typical ADHD behavior such as interrupting others, lack of eye contact, hyperactivity, an inability to notice social cues, and lack of confidence can make children with ADHD easy targets for teasing and bullying. Be sure to use praise to counteract any negative perceptions your child may develop because of this.

Role-playing at home is crucial. Work with your child on maintaining eye contact, using transitional expressions such as "Hi," "Bye," and "See ya" when meeting or leaving friends, the importance of common courtesy, and saying "Please," "Thank you," and "I'm sorry" when necessary.

Encourage your child to count to ten in his head before making any comments or trying to participate in a conversation. This will help him avoid blurting out inappropriate things and help him become a better listener. Closely monitor social media use as well, and teach him to think through posts and comments he makes before posting them.

If your tween doesn't understand why he gets such negative attention, he may conclude that he's basically and hopelessly unlikable and simply withdraw. Kids can be cruel and thoughtless, but it's important not to dismiss the situation, especially if you have a child with ADHD.

Work with your child on developing social skills that make him less of a target. Praise him when he has a successful encounter with a bully, and encourage him to seek out friends who respect and like him. It may also help to tell him about your own tween struggles with teasers and bullies.

Parental Involvement in Extracurricular Activities

Most parents agree that one of the best ways to improve a child with ADHD's academic and social success is to get involved in some way in her school. Studies indicate that the children of parents who are involved at their school tend to get better grades, have fewer behavior problems, have better relationships with their teachers and classmates, and grow up to become more responsible adults. When you participate in your child's school, you're giving your child a message that her school is important to you.

By participating at your child's school, you'll also get a better idea of who your child's friends are, and your child will be less likely to get bullied or teased. You'll also get to know your child's teachers better.

Can Your Adolescent "Grow Out" of ADHD?

Until the early 1990s, scientists considered ADHD a "childhood disorder" and believed that most children outgrew the condition. For that reason, physicians usually took children off medication before they reached high school. In many cases, teenagers suffered serious setbacks academically and socially—a clear sign their ADHD symptoms had not abated.

Continued research has shown that ADHD symptoms do not necessarily go away by adolescence. According to the American Academy of Family Physicians, about two-thirds of children with ADHD continue to have symptoms as adults.

If your child's symptoms become less noticeable as he gets older, your physician may recommend taking him off medication to see how he fares. If your child's symptoms of hyperactivity, inattention, and/or impulsivity don't return, it's probably a good sign your child is among the one-third of children who grow out of ADHD. Or your child may only need to take medication a few times a week to keep symptoms in check.

Tweens with ADHD and Learning Disabilities

It is common for tweens with ADHD to be diagnosed with one or more learning disabilities. Most involve language (especially speaking and understanding what is being said) or a specific academic subject (usually reading or math).

SPECIAL EDUCATION SERVICES

If regular classroom teachers cannot accommodate your child's educational needs, special education help may be a good option. Special education services may involve going to a special classroom all day, getting extra help in a particular subject for an hour a week, or anything in between. It may mean having a specially trained teacher come to the regular classroom to work with your child. To qualify for special education, your tween's ADHD symptoms must cause significant learning or behavior problems at school.

If your child is not eligible under special education law, the Section 504 of the Rehabilitation Act of 1973 legally obligates public schools to ensure that children with disabilities have equal access to education. Services under a "504 Plan" can overlap with special education services, but typically they are mostly accommodations (e.g. extended time on tests, breaks during class, etc.) rather than interventions (a special class or instructor for your child). See Chapter 9 for more information about what to do if you think your child needs special help.

MINDFULNESS ACTIVITIES FOR YOUR MIDDLE SCHOOL CHILD

Middle-school-age children have longer attention spans than younger children and are ready for lengthier or more abstract mindfulness activities. They might be ready for five to ten minutes of mindfulness activities at a time. The key is to be playful and experimental about the mindfulness activities you try with your child, instead of making it a chore or something she has to do. Here are some suggestions:

O Mindful music activities are a good place to start with your middle schooler. Put on a song of her choice and listen to the song together, focusing on the lyrics, the instruments used, the pitch, tone, and other musical aspects.

O Begin to teach comfortable mindfulness meditation poses, such as sitting in a chair with feet flat on the ground, hands on the lap, and straight, yet comfortable posture. Or, try sitting with crossed legs on a pillow, or lying down with arms and legs uncrossed. In these poses, you can have your child do deep breathing or guided meditation using an app from your smartphone. For a good list of resources, check out *http://kidsrelaxation.com*.

O "Green time" instead of "screen time" can be a good way for your child to practice mindfulness in nature. As you walk with your child, have her listen for sounds, be aware of smells, and try to find something new that you haven't seen before on your walk.

O Middle school students can journal or draw about their experiences with learning new mindfulness skills as a way to increase their self-awareness. They can ask themselves what mindfulness activity did they try? How did it feel to do it? What got in the way of being mindful? Would they be willing to try the activity again?

O Middle school students may also enjoy using mindfulness apps on their smartphones as a way to begin practicing mindfulness. Apps such as Headspace, Breathe2Relax, and Stop, Breathe & Think are good places to start.

O The loving-kindness meditation is a good one for middle school tweens, who may be inundated with negative peer interactions. During this activity, you "send" loving-kindness or friendly wishes to yourself or others. You can model this for your child and take turns sending/thinking friendly or positive wishes to others. Children can start with themselves, friends, or people who have hurt them ("I wish this person to be happy," or "I wish the person I am picturing to be less angry," or "May I be safe and happy.")

The loving-kindness meditation, sometimes called "metta meditation," is rooted in Buddhist practice, and it is essentially the practice of developing compassion. The practice aims to cultivate appreciation and love for one's self and others. Research shows that this type of meditation can increase positive emotions and more satisfaction in life and in relationships.

O Continue mindfulness rituals throughout the day. Have your child pick one activity she always does (e.g. walk to school, eat lunch, clean her room, put on her pajamas, etc.) and be mindful during that moment. Being mindful means that she thinks about only the activity she is doing and how it feels. When her mind drifts to another thought, have her gently bring it back to the sensory aspect of the activity.

Recent studies show that the more present people are during the day, the happier they are. It is easy to get caught up in thinking about things or conversations that have happened, or in planning ahead for what is going to happen. You can often forget to live in the moment. The moment doesn't need to be positive to get the happiness benefit. What is important is being mindful and present no matter what the moment brings.

Important Points to Consider

Here are a few points to remember as your child moves through his tween years:

1. Middle school is an important and difficult time in your child's life. Encourage her to handle her stress through meditation and other mindfulness exercises.

2. Talk to your child's teachers and principal. Open communication with these key people can help you and your child deal with challenges.

3. If your child is showing aversion to school, try getting involved in some extracurricular activities with him. Being present and in the moment with your child can show him that school is important and should be taken seriously.

4. Role-playing is a great way to spend time with your child and to help her practice her social cues.

5. If your child is going through a difficult time at school, acknowledge her struggle, but don't dwell on it. Before you immediately give ideas about ways to make things better for your tween, ask her if she wants you to simply listen to her struggles or if she wants you to brainstorm some ideas together about what to do. Sometimes tweens just need to be heard, and other times they need problem solving.

6. Routines are more than just a way to ease anxiety for you and your tween. Keeping a steady routine with homework and bedtime can help your tween learn to judge how much time it will take him to complete certain tasks.

CHAPTER 6

ADHD in Teenagers

High school means coping with academic challenges on top of raging hormones, peer pressure, and sexuality. Add ADHD to the mix, and the transition from childhood to adulthood can be especially trying. As a conscious parent, you can help your teen with ADHD weather his high school years by being calm and supportive, and keeping an honest dialogue with your teen open at all times. Understand that sometimes your teen may not want to engage with you, but always be present with him in the moment, even if that moment is full of silence. Your unwavering support throughout his teen years will give him strength in the future. Your presence will also help him build the strong organizational skills he needs for academic success, and the strong social skills he needs to master relationships with friends, teachers, and the opposite sex.

Dealing with Academic/ Classroom Challenges

The three major symptoms of ADHD—hyperactivity, impulsiveness, and inattention—may also wreak havoc on a teenager's ability to function at school. Many high school students with ADHD have difficulty sitting still, listening, and staying focused. They also experience problems with executive functions such as taking and organizing notes, comprehending reading and homework assignments, and getting to class on time. In addition, they may fail to turn in homework assignments or complete projects by the deadline.

MASTERING EXECUTIVE FUNCTIONS

For many teens with ADHD, the biggest academic challenge is handling and mastering the wide range of executive functions required of them by teachers and professors. This includes organizing, prioritizing, delegating, planning, meeting deadlines, and conceptualizing long-range plans and goals.

Staying focused is probably the biggest executive challenge for teens with ADHD. That's because to get anything accomplished, you have to initiate, stay focused, concentrate, and stick with it until it's finished.

Without focus, the end result is that the project or task doesn't get done on time—or at all. High school students with ADHD often have to work late on homework and projects, and even devote entire weekends to completing them. Others become so distracted that, despite high IQs, they fail subjects or drop out of school. Studies show high school students with ADHD are more likely to drop out of school, flunk out of college, and perform below their academic abilities than other teens.

STRATEGIES TO IMPROVE EXECUTIVE FUNCTIONS

Unfortunately, teens with ADHD often find it difficult to pay attention, especially when they find the subject boring, dull, repetitive, or uninteresting. Instead of focusing, their minds wander. This is where mindful practices can come in handy. Teach your child the benefits of meditation, deep breathing, and being present in the moment—these are skills he can draw on when he is having trouble focusing.

Teaching your child executive functioning skills can go a long way toward preventing school failure. For example, teaching your child strategies for organization, time management, planning ahead for long-term projects, anticipating challenges and making a plan to overcome them, and teaching strategies for starting work that is uninteresting to her are all valuable tools for your child's success.

Does Medication Give Your Teen an Academic Edge?

ADHD medications are powerful drugs that can enhance mental abilities, improve clarity, and enhance awareness in children with ADHD, as well as in children who don't have the disorder. That said, if your child suffers from ADHD, he may need to take stimulant medication to correct brain malfunctions that can lead to underperformance and social problems. In other words, stimulant medication will not give your child with ADHD an academic edge so much as help him to perform as he would without the disorder.

Unfortunately, people who don't suffer from ADHD often abuse ADHD drugs. According to *Wired* magazine, many top performers in academic and technology fields abuse these drugs, either through prescriptions or from friends, to get an extra competitive edge. Parents and even some professionals are also guilty of giving ADHD drugs to students who don't suffer from the condition to enhance their academic performance at school.

Your child may prefer to hide the fact that he takes stimulant medications for his ADHD. Teens and college students who don't have ADHD and take these medications illegally are categorized as drug abusers, and your child may not want to tell others he takes medication for fear he'll suffer the same stigma.

In addition, some high school students with ADHD who take ADHD drugs legally for symptoms feel they must hide the fact they take stimulant medications so their friends and peers won't pressure them to share or sell their drugs to them.

Helping Your Teen Get and Stay Organized

Disorganization is a classic symptom of ADHD, and it can make it difficult for your teen to do many tasks at school. Your child may have trouble getting things done on time, prioritizing, breaking up large tasks into small doable pieces, keeping track of books and materials for different classes, and even remembering what classroom to go to at what time.

Here are some strategies you can encourage your high school student with ADHD to adopt to get and stay organized in school. Remember, don't nag her to become more organized.

- ○ Centralize important information. Use a desk calendar, personal organization system, or computer calendar that syncs with her smartphone to keep all her essential dates, appointments, reminders, to-do lists, and deadlines in one central location.

- ○ Buy an easy-to-use filing system with color-coded folders to organize her important projects into separate tasks. Don't use manila envelopes, as materials may fall out of the sides and get lost in the shuffle. Consider using one binder with tabs instead of multiple folders to streamline the organization process.

- ○ Have a daily "clearing the decks" ritual. Have her declutter her desk, file important documents, and clear out and file materials in her in- and outboxes. If something is urgent, have her tackle it immediately before she forgets about it or gets distracted.

Helping Your Child Deal with Anger and Criticism

Teen ADHD symptoms may inhibit your child's ability to appropriately interact with others at school or work, be a good team player, handle criticism, deal with authority figures, and conduct himself appropriately during class or with friends. These factors often play a significant role in how teachers and mentors perceive him, and can be the difference between him getting ahead and falling behind.

MANAGING EMOTIONS

Many teens with ADHD have fragile egos. If your child's self-esteem is wobbly, he may need to be especially careful about acting defensive, continually putting himself down, or letting other people's perceptions or opinions of him affect his conduct.

Instead of letting a bad temper or inappropriate comments jeopardize his schoolwork or job, have your teen role-play managing his temper and communicating thoughts to others instead of keeping them bottled up.

MANAGING THE EFFECTS OF LOW SELF-ESTEEM

Many teens with ADHD have low self-esteem, and this can manifest at school in a variety of negative ways that can be detrimental to establishing, maintaining, or advancing their careers. For instance, low self-esteem may cause your teen to be overly concerned about or sensitive to what others think or feel about him, and cause him to put more time and energy into worrying than working.

Your teen's low self-esteem may cause him to be very self-critical, defensive when it comes to accepting criticism, or angry because he feels he isn't valued or appreciated. A therapist can help your teen uncover some of the reasons or dysfunctional thinking behind his poor self-esteem and help him look for ways to improve or bolster it.

DEALING WITH AUTHORITY FIGURES

Many teens with ADHD have trouble dealing with authority figures including teachers, professors, and bosses. Many teens with ADHD simply believe they are right about everything most of the time—despite all evidence to the contrary—and that other people are wrong most of the time. Before your teen lets his stubbornness get the best of him, encourage him to consider the possibility that he could actually be wrong this time (or any time).

If your teen still thinks he's right and his teacher or boss is wrong, encourage him to think carefully about what he would accomplish by confronting his teacher or boss, taking into consideration his personal track record and his personal relationship with the authority figure. Would the teacher or boss be likely to listen and thank your teen for his input, or be so impressed by your teen's insight that he'd change his mind? Or would he be more likely to be annoyed and insulted that your teen had the nerve to defy him and, in turn, give him a low grade?

DISCOVERING YOUR TEEN'S ACADEMIC STRENGTHS AND WEAKNESSES

ADHD can hamper your teen's ability to look at himself realistically and gauge his strengths and weaknesses. Not knowing what he's good at (or bad at) can have an impact on his academic and job performance in many ways. He may struggle with a subject, major, or career path that doesn't match his innate talents, or become bored, disgruntled, or disappointed when his efforts don't yield the results he had expected.

You can help him keep a healthy perspective by offering support and praise. Eventually he will begin to see positive aspects in himself without your help.

A good therapist can help your teen home in on his strengths and weaknesses so he can minimize shortcomings and maximize his many gifts. Many teens with ADHD decide to change college majors after working with a therapist and wind up on different career paths that better fit their ADHD skills and temperaments.

Dating, Networking, and Other Social Challenges

Dating can tax the social skills of a fragile teen with ADHD to the breaking point. Consider sitting down with your teen to take inventory of her social strengths and weaknesses so she can avoid dating situations that are likely to become awkward or stressful.

DATING

Encourage your teen to avoid dating situations that will stress her out because they require maintaining strict focus during lengthy and/or complex conversations. Better bets for dates for teens who have ADHD include social activities that do not revolve around passively listening and watching rather than actively participating (such as seeing a movie or a play).

SOCIAL MEDIA CHALLENGES

Much of teenager's social life, including dating, takes place online through social media sites. The unwritten rules of what to post and what not to post are not explicitly taught, and a teenager who doesn't always think through her actions may need some guidance. You can save your teen from a social faux pas and heartache if you have her subscribe to a few simple rules:

- If you wouldn't say something to a person's face, don't post it on social media.

- If you wouldn't say something to every student in school, don't post it on social media.

- Never post pictures you wouldn't want your parents, teachers, or future employers to see. Everything you post has a permanent digital fingerprint.

- Before you post anything, re-read your post and ask yourself, "Could this be interpreted as hurtful by anyone?" or "How does this post make me look to others?" If there is even a small chance it could be interpreted as hurtful or it makes you look insensitive, don't post it.

HANDLING SOCIAL CHALLENGES

Everyone needs friends, especially teenagers with ADHD. If your child's symptoms have made it difficult or challenging for her to make meaningful friendships and maintain them during troubled times, she may be going about it in the wrong way. Here are some strategies to help her make and keep friendships that can sustain her through good times and bad.

Encourage your teen to pick her activities carefully. Your teen is already working hard enough to pay attention, focus, concentrate, and read nonverbal cues without forcing herself to do something she dislikes. Engaging in an activity she doesn't enjoy will only cause her to get bored, tune out, or drift away.

Encourage your teen to practice being a friend. Making and keeping friends requires time and effort on your teen's part, so make sure she doesn't expect friendships to flourish in a vacuum. Your teen can make staying in touch with friends easy and fast by creating a master list of names, phone numbers, and e-mail addresses on the computer. Have her set aside some time every week to touch base with close friends and set up lunch dates or activities with those that live nearby.

Encourage your teen to contact more casual friends and acquaintances about once a month to keep the connection going. If she has limited time for staying in touch, tell her that it's better to make a quick phone call or send a friendly text than to do nothing at all. Her friends are probably as busy as she is, and will likely appreciate that she thought of them.

Encourage your teen to surprise friends on important dates in their lives by sending a card, birthday text/post, flowers, candy, or special gift. Your child's thoughtfulness in remembering birthdays, anniversaries, and special occasions will go a long way toward cementing relationships.

ADHD and Addictions

Research shows that teenagers with undiagnosed ADHD may be walking time bombs on a variety of levels. Compared to teenagers without the disorder, teenagers with ADHD are twice as likely to run away from home, three times as likely to be arrested, ten times as likely to get pregnant or cause a pregnancy, and 400 times as likely to contract a sexually transmitted disease. Engage your teen in conversations about risks and the importance of thinking through her behaviors.

Many teenagers with ADHD have a penchant for risky behavior as well as a need for constant stimulation. It's no mystery why some of them turn to alcohol or drugs for kicks. Research shows that teens with undiagnosed ADHD are especially prone to drug use because they may be attempting to self-medicate themselves with illegal drugs that bear a resemblance to ADHD drugs. Other children with ADHD abuse drugs or alcohol to mask symptoms of social discomfort or phobias. Talk to your child about the dangers of alcohol and drug abuse and be on the lookout for warning signs.

Is Your Teen Safe Behind the Wheel?

Most parents worry when their teens reach driving age, and when a teen has ADHD, fears escalate. Car accidents are the number one cause of death for teenagers. Studies show that about 63 percent of those killed are drivers, and 37 percent are passengers. Drivers with ADHD who are in their teen years face a double whammy when it comes to being safe behind the wheel: They have limited experience dealing with driving challenges, and they also lack the maturity required to make good judgment calls.

> Teenagers with impulsive ADHD are also a hazard behind the wheel and have a 400 percent greater risk of being in traffic accidents than other teens.

Teenagers with ADHD also have a "no fear" attitude that can translate into reckless behavior behind the wheel. Coupled with ADHD symptoms of inattention, impulsivity, lack of focus, and an inability to stop and think before acting, it's no mystery why teenage drivers with ADHD are at the top of the list when it comes to fatal car accidents.

STRATEGIES FOR PARENTS

If your teenager wants to drive, sit down with him and discuss the effects his lack of driving ability can have on increasing his risk of accidents. Help him develop strategies that will reduce his chances of having car accidents, and make sure he understands that driving is a privilege that can be revoked at any time.

Go on practice rides with your teen to let him improve his driving skills under your supervision. You'll have a better idea of how well he drives, and what he needs to improve in order to reduce his risk of causing an accident. Make sure your teen understands the dangers of driving while talking on the cell phone, texting, changing music, or listening to music or the radio while driving, and limit nighttime driving until you've taken several test drives with your teen. You may also want to set some ground rules about how many passengers your teen can have in the car at the same time to reduce the risk of distractions.

DRIVING WITHOUT MEDICATION

Many teens with ADHD refuse to take their medication because they don't like the side effects, and/or because they consider ADHD a social stigma and don't want to be associated with the disorder or medications prescribed for it. If your teen wants to discontinue medication, you may want to put off letting her drive until you see how she fares without medication. If her symptoms worsen or remain severe, you may want to prohibit her from driving until she's back on medication and her ADHD symptoms are under control.

Teenage ADHD Rebellion

The teenage years are a normal time of rebellion for any teen. But teens with ADHD are far more likely to be rebellious than other teens because of the core symptoms of the disorder. Because they need constant stimulation and excitement, many teens with ADHD are drawn to risky behaviors such as truancy, drinking, and drug use. If your teen is experimenting with or engaging in risky behaviors and you need help, seek out a professional. Chapter 15 describes the types of therapy that may be beneficial for your teen.

Helping Your Teen Get Into College or Find a Career Path

Every college or university with federal funding is obligated to provide "reasonable accommodations" for the estimated 2–4 percent of college students who have ADHD, but the amount of help varies widely among schools.

Some colleges provide the bare minimum to comply with the federal law. Others offer every imaginable service to accommodate students with adult ADHD, including student disability services, study skills programs, specialized help during registration and freshman orientation, on-campus physicians who specialize in treating ADHD, and access to on-campus ADHD coaches, counseling, psychotherapy, and support groups.

If your child has ADHD, you may want to help him look for a college or university that has a welcoming and supportive attitude toward students with the disorder. The college your child chooses should go out of its way to facilitate his transition from high school to college life. Have your child work with his high school guidance counselor or hire a private college counselor to home in on colleges that have small class sizes, low student-to-professor ratios, and an emphasis on personalized attention.

TO DISCLOSE OR NOT TO DISCLOSE

Although there is no law dictating that your child must disclose that he has ADHD, it's often a wise choice. By disclosing his disability, your child will provide the admissions department with the information they need to make an informed decision about how well he's likely to fit in at their school. Your child may also be eligible for valuable assistance through the college's disabilities office.

College students diagnosed with ADHD may be eligible for services under Section 504 of the Rehabilitation Act of 1973 and the Americans with Disabilities Act. If your child decides to disclose that he has ADHD, he will be required to submit documentation of his disorder. This may include records of psychological evaluations, the date of diagnosis, high school records that document special assistance he received, and a current Individualized Education Program.

Once your child has decided on a college, he should register for disabilities services right away. To ensure he'll get the services he needs from the start, he should apply for admissions and disabilities services at the same time.

College students with ADHD may qualify for the use of assisted technology to help them cope with their disability. These include voice-activated software, audiobooks, personal organizers, and computer outlining programs.

SPECIAL CHALLENGES FOR STUDENTS WITH ADHD

In college, most of your child's life will revolve around being able to concentrate, focus, retain knowledge, take good notes, schedule time for studying, and manage his time so that he gets things done on time. For this reason, typical ADHD problems with executive functions can present a unique challenge to college students with ADHD.

Many students with ADHD overestimate what they can realistically accomplish in one semester. Others, away from the day-to-day assistance of parents and family for the first time in their lives, become overwhelmed with the number of decisions and choices facing them.

TIPS FOR COLLEGE SUCCESS

To ensure your child's college experience is a positive one, make sure you and your child plan ahead. Have him address his inherent limitations and map out a plan of action to deal with them. Make sure your child has access to learning services and academic support to help reduce stress and frustration.

If your child has significant problems with executive functions, you may want to hire an ADHD coach who can help him organize his time and establish good study habits. Joining an ADHD support group or peer study group on campus may help your child make meaningful friendships, help him feel more hooked into campus life, and give him a safe place to vent his fears and frustrations. If the college has a student health center, encourage your child to introduce himself to the physician on staff.

Mindfulness Activities for Teenagers

Getting your teenager to "buy in" to doing mindfulness activities may be the hardest part of the process. She may not think it's "cool" or may resist it simply because a parent is suggesting it. You can share the research on how mindful students do better in school, have improved concentration, increased happiness, and fewer symptoms of depression or anxiety. You can also enlist other people, such as her school guidance counselor, a therapist, a trusted teacher, an older sibling or family member, or an ADHD coach, to encourage her to try mindfulness activities. Teenagers want to feel independent, so providing your teen with a choice of different activities that may resonate with her is important. Acknowledge any reservations she may have and encourage her to be experimental and see if anything "sticks."

A good place to start to show the promising results of mindfulness and get ideas for how to get started on a core practice that works for your teen is the Greater Good Science Center at *http://greatergood.berkeley.edu*.

O Encourage ten minutes of tech-free time each day to do a mindfulness activity, such as taking a walk, eating a snack, or meditating. If you are also prone to tech addiction, you can practice this activity with your teen and then discuss what it was like to disconnect.

O Use interest in technology to your advantage by looking for mindfulness apps to download and use, such as Headspace, Smiling Mind, Take a Break!, or Stop, Breathe & Think. Sign on to these apps yourself and experiment with them together (not necessarily at the same time of day).

O Your teen may also enjoy using the camera on her phone as a tool for mindfulness. She could take a photo each day of something that makes her life seem meaningful, or things/people she is grateful for or in awe of, and review them at the end of the week. "Selfies" may be fun too; have your teen look outward and reflect on the positive aspects of her life.

O Many teens have a hard time unwinding at bedtime. This is a good opportunity to build in a mindfulness ritual, in which your teen plays relaxing music, nature sounds, or a guided imagery right before bedtime.

O Encourage your teenager to explore the "right" mindfulness activity for her. Refer her to websites such as *http://mindfulnessforteens.com* or have her look on Pinterest for mindfulness activities or mantras she can use for meditation.

○ Encourage exercise that incorporates mindfulness, such as yoga, martial arts, or "ecstatic dance" classes (dancing without choreography or self-judgment).

Important Points to Consider

Being a teenager can be difficult. As your teen grows, encourage her to keep the line of communication open between the two of you. Your goal is to listen and be present as much as possible. Here are a few other things to remember during your child's teen years:

1. Staying focused is a difficult task for teens with ADHD. When you see your teen struggling, offer support and encouragement, and be sure to praise her when the task is complete.

2. If your child struggles with self-esteem, reminding her how unique and special she is can help refocus her attention. It may also be a good idea to seek out a therapist that specializes in teens with ADHD to help your teen control her emotions.

3. You can help him keep a healthy perspective by offering support and praise. Eventually he will begin to see positive aspects in himself without your help.

4. Remember that your teen's low self-esteem may cause him to be very self-critical, defensive when it comes to accepting criticism, or angry because he feels he isn't valued or appreciated. If you find yourself in a situation where your teen is acting out, take a deep breath and center yourself. Do not react with anger, or things may get even more heated.

5. Teens are sometimes rebellious by nature. Part of being a conscious parent is keeping a dialogue with your child going at all times so he feels comfortable coming to you with questions and concerns. It is important to talk to your child about the dangers of alcohol and drug abuse and to be on the lookout for warning signs.

 **CHAPTER 7**

Creating Harmony at Home

Sometimes childhood ADHD can turn the happiest home into a never-ending battlefront. Core symptoms of disorganization, distraction, inattention, and impulsivity can unravel the fabric of family life and cause emotional, mental, physical, and financial turmoil for everyone involved. You may even find that you are often stretched to the breaking point in your attempt to raise children and manage household affairs. At these times, being mindful might be the last thing you want to do, but don't give up. Conscious parenting is about being present with your child, no matter the circumstance. Before you reach the end of your rope, take a few moments to pause and reflect on your feelings. Are you really angry with your child or are you just frustrated with your current situation? Simply acknowledge that you are human and move on. The following chapter offers lots of tips and strategies for creating a happy home life when one or more of your children have ADHD.

Helping Family Members Manage ADHD

Ask anyone who suffers from it, or anyone who lives with a sufferer, and you'll probably get the same response: At times, it can seem that childhood ADHD is synonymous with conflict and disruption. The disorder often creates nonstop chaos and havoc in practically every area and aspect of the home.

> Being a parent is hard enough without adding in ADHD. Even the most organized and efficient parents can end the day feeling overwhelmed, confused, and exhausted when dealing with a child who has ADHD. That is perfectly normal. Part of conscious parenting is cutting yourself some slack. You are trying the best you can.

THE STAR IN HER OWN SOAP OPERA

Because ADHD is often accompanied by emotional and behavioral volatility, the condition itself makes the child prone to drama. As most family members can appreciate, including the sufferer herself, it's not usually the sort of drama anyone would buy a ticket to see.

One way parents or siblings can pull the plug on ADHD-inspired soap operas is to sit down with a family therapist and get to the bottom of why the child with ADHD feels compelled to spin out soap operas. Once the sufferer and her family members understand the emotional voids the dramas are intended to fill, they can help boost her self-esteem, increase her confidence, and replace her energy-draining dramas with more productive activities that can strengthen rather than deflate her resources, and improve family morale.

UNDERSTANDING AND RECOGNIZING THE ROOT OF MOOD SWINGS

In addition to her constant need for drama, a child with ADHD is also likely to suffer from periodic or chronic mood swings. It's important for family members to understand that these mood swings are often not connected to or triggered by a particular event or person, but may be the result of neurobiological imbalances, waxing and waning medication levels, side effects of medications, dietary triggers, and coexisting depression or anxiety.

Children with ADHD are often extremely sensitive to criticism and may put up a wall to protect themselves from what may feel like a never-ending barrage. Having disappointed many people over time, and having been told countless times they are unpredictable, unreliable, or unproductive, they may react to similar complaints from family members by withdrawing or lashing back.

Exhaustion from having to cope with a daily parade of symptoms can also make children with ADHD feel helpless, scared, and hopeless. A family therapist can work with family members and the child to take a closer look at mood swings, help isolate likely triggers, eliminate possible causes, and educate the family about mood triggers that may not always be treatable.

LETTING GO OF THE PAST

Many children and teenagers with ADHD live with perpetual feelings of guilt and shame about failures of the past, even if their failures were triggered by undiagnosed ADHD symptoms and not caused by their lack of motivation, laziness, lack of productivity, or disinterest. Like a broken record, the song of "failure" plays itself over and over again and often drowns out present-day successes and accomplishments.

By working with a family therapist and by focusing on living in the present, family members can help the child with ADHD understand that until she stops dwelling on past failures and begins to live in the present, she will never begin to replace her gloom-and-doom with feelings of contentment and happiness. Once she realizes it's impossible to undo the past and that the more she feeds it negative thoughts, the longer she keeps it alive, a child or teen with ADHD can bury the past and open her eyes to the many possibilities, opportunities, and avenues for joy that exist in the present. Once you're successfully managing your child's ADHD symptoms, you can begin to incorporate some basic ground rules of parenting that will help keep things running smoothly on the home front.

Many children with ADHD suffer from depression and anxiety. Living with a gloom-and-doom pessimist who seems hardwired for continued failure can gradually wear down and pollute the spirits of the sunniest family members and cause them to resent the "downer" in their midst. Mindfulness has a double benefit of targeting attention problems and depression; try to infuse mindfulness activities into the family routines so all family members can decrease stress.

SEVEN STRATEGIES FOR QUIETING CHAOS IN THE HOME

Here are some strategies that will help you and other family members become more consistent and loving parents and siblings:

1. Keep it consistent. Consistency is probably not one of your child's strong suits if she suffers from inattention and has trouble focusing. As a parent, it's important to keep things consistent so your child doesn't get confused or frustrated. As the parent of a child with ADHD, you need to be consistent about everything from house rules to serving meals. Be consistent, too, about disciplining your children so they understand that your "no" this time will also be a "no" next time, and not a "maybe" or a "yes."

2. Keep it organized. Again, this is probably not one of your child's strong suits, but an ADHD coach may be your best resource in helping organize the household schedule, finances, and chores. As explained in the last chapter, one strategy that works for many parents of children with ADHD is posting a family calendar of events and commitments.

3. Lose the Supermom (or Superdad) cape. As the parent of a child with ADHD, don't set unrealistically high expectations for yourself or your child. Don't commit to more than you or she can do, or both you and your child will feel frustrated, guilty, disappointed in yourselves, and overwhelmed. If you're overbooking your child's schedule, it won't take long before something falls through the cracks and your child either forgets or doesn't have time to do something very important. Don't hesitate to delegate.

4. Create and stick to simple daily routines. The thought of creating and following set routines may be enough to give your child hives, but without set routines, your home life will resemble chaos in no time. To get the day started on the right foot, create a weekday morning routine for you and your child. Create set routines for after school and evening that include after-school snacks and exercise, eating together as a family, and completing homework assignments. Add a family mindfulness ritual to your daily routine so it becomes a way of being instead of a "to-do" item.

5. Set alarms to help you remember appointments, deadlines, and to take dinner out of the oven. Your child already has a tendency to get hyperfocused on one thing and forget about everything else. To make it easy for your child to remember important things, set kitchen timers or alarms on smartphones so they beep or buzz to remind her.

6. Create a Grand Central Station for anything that family members use on a daily basis. This will prevent these items from getting scattered around the house or lost in space. To make it easy to keep things organized, build cubbies for your child's backpacks and outerwear. Install a key rack by the door for car and house keys (and keep duplicate sets in a different location). Designate a special place in the house for eyeglasses, sunglasses, wallets, purses, and phones. Every object should have a "home."

7. Accentuate the positive. Remember that children with ADHD are like litmus paper and will absorb any negative vibes you put out there. If you catch yourself feeling chronically depressed or negative, remember to count your blessings and focus on your gifts, and you'll teach your child with ADHD to do the same thing.

Remember that mindfulness activities can help reduce your stress, which makes you a better, more patient parent. Find time to dedicate to a core practice, even if it is only ten minutes a day, to recharge so you will have positive energy for your child. See Chapter 8 for information about learning your own core mindfulness practice.

Handling Disruptive Behavior

Regardless of how childhood ADHD may have unraveled your family or marriage in the past, it's possible to do damage control and get things in order. Get everyone in the family to master some basic coping techniques and skills aimed at helping the child with ADHD help himself and prevent inflicting chaos on others.

TRY A LITTLE TENDERNESS

Ask family members to try to put themselves in the child with ADHD's place. Until everyone in the family understands that their sibling or child with ADHD isn't intentionally screwing up, forgetting to show up, failing to pay attention, or neglecting to listen, they will assume that he is doing it on purpose to make them angry or upset, because he doesn't care, because he's disinterested in what they are doing, or for a million other imaginary reasons.

Practice the loving-kindness meditation with your child as the focal person. Send your child loving thoughts such as "I wish him calmness and happiness" or "May he learn new skills each day so he can feel better about himself." This meditation may help you remember to be empathetic toward your child's difficulties. You can also use the loving-kindness meditation with yourself as the focal person before you go to bed, instead of reflecting on all the parenting mistakes you might have made in the day (e.g. "May I be a positive and happy parent.")

ACKNOWLEDGE AND RELEASE PENT-UP FEELINGS

Another strategy families can use to weather the unpredictable symptoms and emotions of children with ADHD is to agree to acknowledge and share how things make them feel, rather than bottling them up and letting things fester.

Instead of feeling increasingly frustrated with your child with ADHD's inability to do a simple chore, you can acknowledge his ADHD shortcomings—including his own frustration at not being able to get his chore done on time—and help him devise a strategy that can help him master the task next time.

One general strategy that can help alleviate conflicts on the home front is to ensure that all family members recognize their child or sibling with ADHD is operating with some basic mental and emotional deficiencies that make doing simple things very difficult for him. By having compassion for him and adjusting their expectations and demands so he can succeed, everyone wins.

Effective Intervention Strategies

Maybe you feel guilty because your child with ADHD forgot to do her homework or insulted her teacher or a classmate. Or perhaps you're embarrassed that your child blurted out something confidential and potentially embarrassing at a family get-together.

Regardless of who feels guilt and shame regarding ADHD symptoms, it's important for the entire family to recognize that the child with ADHD is not doing it on purpose—he is doing the best he can with the skill set he has at this moment in time.

Instead of blaming, family members can help the child or sibling with ADHD mend her ways by helping her get more organized by creating family calendars, schedules, and timetables. You can also help her to stay more focused on conversations by teaching active listening skills such as periodically reflecting back to a speaker what she has said and to rein in impulsive behavior and comments by counting to ten before saying something potentially insulting or embarrassing.

HELPING CHILDREN WITH ADHD GET ORGANIZED

One way to keep a child with ADHD organized is to display prominent schedules and timetables at strategic locations throughout the house. Rather than hiding schedules in computer files that are only obvious when opened, post duplicate schedules in the kitchen, in the bedroom, on bathroom mirrors—wherever family members will see them repeatedly and be likely to remember them.

PRACTICING THANKS AND GRATITUDE

Everyone needs to be appreciated, acknowledged, and thanked for their accomplishments, achievements, and attempts—especially children with ADHD who are so accustomed to being criticized and slammed that they are hardwired for blame, accusations, and negativity. You can practice gratitude as a family at the dinner table, or right before bedtime by saying one thing about a family member that you appreciate. This will help your child focus on the positive interactions throughout the day and "file" them away, alongside the more challenging moments.

It's also amazing what a little humor can do to defuse a potentially embarrassing or difficult situation. Instead of focusing on the negative ("You forgot to pick up the take-out pizza on your way home from school, and now it's probably too soggy and cold to eat!") lighten up and reframe it as a funny episode that will go down in time in the family scrapbook.

Work with a Therapist to Improve Communication

Miscommunications between family members can have dire consequences. Failing to communicate about where your child with ADHD is going or what time he needs to be picked up could leave your child stranded in a dangerous place or situation without supervision.

A family therapist with experience in dealing with ADHD can help your family work on strategies to prevent communication snafus and make sure that everyone in the family understands the limitations imposed by childhood ADHD. A therapist can also help everyone find ways to overcome the communication gaps that can lead to anger, frustration, resentment, and hurt feelings, and which can create potentially uncomfortable or even dangerous situations in the home.

Another technique your therapist may have you and family members practice is resisting the temptation to criticize. Criticism tends to reduce or shut down communication by building walls or creating conflicts that disguise the real issue at hand.

Children with ADHD are so weary of being criticized, ridiculed, and blamed for doing things wrong they may shut down if you or family members begin your conversation with criticism or negativity. A family therapist can teach family members to set the stage for open communication by beginning every conversation with something they enjoy and appreciate about their child or sibling with ADHD.

It cannot be said enough—the more you take care of yourself, the better parent you will be. Practicing mindfulness and non-judgmental awareness of your parenting is the first step toward self-care. When you take care of yourself, you have more mental energy, optimism, and enthusiasm when the going gets tough. Dedicate yourself to a core mindfulness practice, even if it is only for a few moments in the day.

Important Points to Consider

Part of being a successful parent is understanding that sometimes things are out of your control. It is important to be flexible and to practice nonjudgmental awareness of your limits. Here are a few other tips to remember:

1. Give yourself a break. You can't teach your child to be kind to himself if you aren't practicing what you are preaching.

2. Helping your child to let go of any past "failures" will do wonders for boosting self-esteem in the future.

3. Never underestimate the power of a good routine. If your child is feeling out of control, anxious, or depressed, familiarity may help calm her nerves and bring her back to earth.

4. When you start to feel angry or annoyed with your child, remember that he is just as frustrated as you are. Taking the time to imagine how your child is feeling can help you to better understand his behavior.

5. Do *not* blame—not yourself and especially not your child. Resist the urge to be critical as much as possible. Your goal is to help your child enjoy life in the present moment.

CHAPTER 8

The Promise of Mindfulness

Mindfulness is the practice of being attentive in every moment, and noticing what is taking place both inside and outside of you without judgment. It is the practice of purposefully seeing your thoughts, emotions, experiences, and surroundings as they arise. Simply put, mindfulness is the act of paying attention. This may seem easy, but the truth is, this is a difficult task for anyone, especially children with ADHD! Being mindful cultivates awareness and concentration, two incredibly important traits for people of any age. Mindfulness also helps you to practice being present within your life, just as it is, and hopefully to be more intentional about what you do as a result. When you bring mindfulness to your parenting, there is a double benefit—you can be more the parent you want to be, and your child learns from your example. When parents and children alike practice mindfulness, they often experience improved communication, find better behavior management strategies, and have greater appreciation of one another. To begin, it is important to understand the basic parts of mindfulness, and how they can help both your child and you.

What Is Mindfulness?

Research has shown that mindfulness, or the process of narrowing or widening one's focus intentionally, can improve attention and decrease stress. Some have likened mindfulness to "yoga for the mind." Mindfulness is a relatively simple concept that can be understood quite readily. Keep in mind, though, that understanding mindfulness is only part of the process; it is not mindfulness itself. To experience the full benefits of mindfulness practice, you have to make it a part of your daily life so you can learn how to use it creatively and spontaneously.

Mindfulness and meditation are two different (although complementary) things. Mindfulness is a state of paying attention to your inner and outer environments, which is something you can practice throughout each day and in the midst of any activity. Meditation is a special practice, a time you set aside to just be still, breathe, and notice the activity of your mind. One way to think about it is that mindfulness is meditation in motion.

To be able to teach mindfulness to your children, you have to take up the practice yourself and learn how to apply it when you are angry or hurt or tired as well as when you are feeling good. Think of it this way: Somebody can describe to you in fantastic detail what it is like to ride a bicycle, but you can't know what it takes to balance on two wheels or what the wind feels like in your hair until you get up and ride yourself.

Your children learn much more from what you do than from what you say. Ever notice how well-behaved parents tend to have well-behaved children? For your kids to realistically be able to make mindfulness practice a part of their lives, you will need to model it for them in your own life.

Although mindfulness is a simple concept, applying it in daily life can be very challenging. When the world (and your mind) cooperate, it can be easy to enjoy the present moment. When things get complicated, however, it can become very difficult to navigate your life skillfully. It helps to have a reminder. The three pillars of mindfulness offer a simple way to bring yourself back to center in the midst of chaos and confusion.

The three pillars of mindfulness are:

1. Pay Attention

2. Receive Openly

3. Act with Intention

PAY ATTENTION

The very core of mindfulness practice is to pay attention to whatever arises, moment to moment. This includes thoughts, feelings, emotions, sensations in your body, and perceptions of others and of your environment. Obviously it is impossible to take in everything all the time, and that is not the goal. Your mind will naturally focus on things as it notices them; the challenge to you is to recognize what comes into your awareness as it does so. Notice how you move when you take physical action; notice the quality of your voice when you speak; notice not only what you think, but also how you react to the thoughts and feelings that come up. Paying attention is this simple act of noticing, and always looking deeper into the how of what you do.

Sometimes, parents fall into the trap of only paying attention to negative interactions and undesired behavior in their children. It's far easier to notice when you are being interrupted or a rule is being broken by your child, because it can trigger a negative and strong emotion. Being mindful and paying attention to when your child *is* behaving well, engaging in quiet play, starting his homework, or interrupting politely will shift your focus to the positive aspects and allow opportunities to praise your child and feel positive emotions.

RECEIVE OPENLY

When you practice paying attention, you will notice many things both in your mind and in the world around you. No matter what form these things take, the next step in the practice of mindfulness is to receive them openly. Inevitably, judgments will arise in your mind; it is totally natural to have thoughts, feelings, and opinions about the things you see. Notice these too and accept them as well. It is not necessary to act on these thoughts, nor should you treat them in some way as "real," although some of them will inevitably feel that way. They are just thoughts. Try not to let yourself become distracted by anything that arises in your mind, just keep paying attention.

Notice any harsh judgments you may have of yourself as a parent, or of your child's behavior. Thinking negative thoughts does not make them true. Simply notice the thought and like a cloud blowing across the sky in the wind, let it go. This practice will help you become less critical of yourself and your child.

ACT WITH INTENTION

When you receive your thoughts openly and do not judge them, you no longer have to be driven by them. Watching the workings of your mind creates a space in which you can pause and consider before you act. When anger arises, it may be tempting to lash out at a loved one, even if he had nothing to do with what has made you angry. If you notice this angry thought, you can take a moment before acting on it and choose to act differently.

You do not have to be at the mercy of what you think or feel; however, trying to stop your brain from thinking is like trying to stop a frog from hopping. The goal of mindfulness is not to stop thoughts and emotions from coming up; mindfulness is about paying attention to the thoughts and emotions that come up, without being completely swept away by them.

Mindfulness practice can help parents identify "early warning signs" for anger, such as annoyance, impatience, and frustration. By noticing and acknowledging these feelings, you may be able to give pause before acting on them. If you verbalize your feelings out loud in the moment, and utilize a coping strategy, you are modeling for your child how to self-regulate as well (e.g. "I am feeling frustrated because I have asked you to put on your shoes three times now and we are late. I am going to take some deep breaths to relax as you put them on.").

Why Mindfulness Is Important for Children with ADHD

Children with attention difficulties have tons of thoughts racing through their minds, making it difficult to focus on just one thing, such as a homework assignment, reading a chapter in a book, or studying for a test. You can teach your child to quiet his mind by modeling and teaching mindfulness practices for him. All children tend to profit from mindfulness practices, but children with ADHD are particularly good candidates for benefiting from the practice. Mindfulness is important for children with ADHD for a number of reasons, for instance it helps them strengthen emotional awareness, cultivate acceptance, and improve self-regulation.

STRENGTHENING EMOTIONAL AWARENESS

People who do not pay attention to their thoughts and feelings often react abruptly when a feeling takes hold of them. This is particularly true of children, whose prefrontal cortexes (the brain's center of reason, planning ahead, risk assessment, impulse control, and emotional regulation) are still developing. Children with ADHD typically have underdeveloped prefrontal cortexes, and thus are more prone to "go from zero to sixty" in terms of their emotions. Through the practice of mindfulness, you and your child can strengthen your emotional awareness and give yourselves space to choose how you want to respond.

In 2008, neuroscientist Richard J. Davidson, PhD, and his colleagues at the University of Wisconsin–Madison observed that mindfulness practice enhanced the ability of practitioners to cool down their emotions when they got stirred up. The increase in emotional self-control observed by participants in Davidson's study was a result of a cooling of activity in the amygdala, a structure in the limbic system whose activity is closely correlated with negative emotions. Participants in the study also observed an overall reduction in anxiety, stress, and negative moods.

CULTIVATING ACCEPTANCE

For children, mindfulness can be a particularly powerful tool for cultivating acceptance. Children are regularly subjected to all sorts of stressors that they have no power over. Younger children are often entirely subject to the demands of their parents' schedules and are transported back and forth on someone else's timetable, put in groups to play with other kids, etc. School-age children and teenagers are famously trapped between childhood and adulthood.

Regardless of age, a child's life is rife with circumstances she cannot control and may not like. Mindfulness can be a powerful tool to help children accept the circumstances of their lives, regardless of how they feel about those circumstances, and can give them a positive way of dealing with this stress. Although you cannot control many of the things that happen to you in life, you *can* control how you respond to them. Mindfulness is a fantastic tool for working with the thoughts, feelings, and stories that arise in the face of challenging circumstances. By working directly with your reactions to events, it is possible to give yourself some breathing room. Just to be clear, mindfulness is not some silver bullet that can alleviate all the suffering in your life, but it can help you change your relationship to that suffering so that it does not completely eclipse the various joys that are available to you in each moment.

Accepting your lack of control over some situations can be a powerful practice. Research has shown that people who have developed ways of doing so generally experience less stress and are more emotionally stable than those who try to control everything. This can be achieved through spiritual belief or through logical reasoning. Whichever style suits you better, try talking to yourself when you identify something you are trying to control but can't. If you realistically can't do anything about it, why worry?

IMPROVING SELF-REGULATION

Practicing mindfulness can increase the brain's ability to monitor and regulate itself. The repeated practice of mindfulness can create and strengthen neuronal pathways for calmness and focus. Kids and teens live in a distracting world. With technological, social, and internal distractions it is no wonder that kids with ADHD have trouble focusing! Teaching children to pay attention through mindfulness activities improves concentration, memory, and mental focus in other activities.

Does Mindfulness Work?

Mindfulness practice brings with it a host of benefits. In recent years, there has been a wealth of scientific research on the effects of mindfulness on the brain. This research has shown the systemic impact that practicing mindfulness has on the brain, and specific benefits to both mental health and cognitive functioning. Mindfulness is particularly effective when working with anxiety and depression, and also has a positive impact on attention and executive functioning. Research has also shown that the brain is affected structurally as well as functionally, meaning that mindfulness can actually stimulate growth in existing brain cells in specific areas as well as enhance their existing functionality.

In a study done by UCLA's Lisa Kilpatrick, PhD, she and her colleagues found that mindfulness meditation brought about measurable increases in brain connectivity, particularly in the auditory and visual networks of the brain. Participants who learned mindfulness improved their ability to maintain focus and block out distractions.

Kilpatrick's study found that not only does mindfulness help you to be less prone to distraction, it actually enhances your ability to focus on what you choose to give your attention to. This also correlates with improved cognitive functioning and perceptual learning, meaning that mindfulness can help you to be clearer, sharper, and more focused. When the brain can block out distractions and concentrate more steadfastly on what it is doing, it processes information much more efficiently. Imagine how your child could benefit from these effects!

Mindfulness and Executive Functioning

Executive functioning is an umbrella term used to describe a variety of different skills that are often lagging in students with ADHD—planning, organizing, ignoring distractions, shifting and dividing attention, controlling impulses, self-regulating behaviors, thoughts, and feelings, etc.

The Everything® Parent's Guide to Children with Executive Functioning Disorder is a resource available for understanding executive functioning. It also teaches practical strategies to your child to support his development.

Mindfulness practice has been shown to improve executive functioning, particularly regarding attention and inhibition ("stop and think" impulse control skills). When you train your child's brain to focus on one thing, it strengthens her ability to do so in other settings. It's like "working out" the focus center of her brain to make it stronger. Studies, including one conducted by the University of Wisconsin–Madison's Lisa Flook, PhD, and her colleagues, published in the *Journal of Applied School Psychology* in 2010, showed that mindfulness improves "global executive control" as well. This means that many of the executive functions, such as metacognition (thinking about one's learning), working memory, planning and organization, and behavioral regulation are improved with mindfulness.

A study by the University of Amsterdam's Dr. Saskia van der Oord and her colleagues, published in the *Journal of Child and Family Studies* in 2012, showed that mindfulness training for children with ADHD and mindful parenting training for their parents resulted in a significant reduction in ADHD symptoms and an increase of mindful awareness. Indeed, research is mounting that shows mindfulness is one of the most promising nonpharmaceutical interventions for ADHD symptoms.

You should always consult with your dispensing physician or psychiatrist before making decisions about medication. Research in mindfulness is promising, but further studies are needed to see if mindfulness works with all types and severity levels of ADHD. A child with mild ADHD may have a different intervention profile than a child with severe to moderate ADHD.

Making Time for Mindfulness

You might be thinking, "Great! Mindfulness works, but when am I going to have time to do mindfulness and teach it to my child?" The good news is that by doing your own mindfulness practice, you are teaching your child by example. Also, you can integrate mindfulness into your daily life, because it is a state of mind, and not necessarily something you have to "do."

As you go about your day, you can simply pay attention to what you are doing while you are doing it (e.g. brushing your teeth, taking a shower, washing the dishes). As soon as you notice your mind has wandered from the sensation of the task (which is normal), gently return your attention to what you are doing. You can teach your child to do the same thing by having her pick a daily activity she always does and to practice thinking about only that activity while she's doing it (e.g. when riding the bus, she can think about the sensation of the bus bouncing up and down, the feel of the breeze on her face from the window, the sounds of the other children talking, or the feeling of her legs on the seat and her feet on the floor). It is less important which task you or your child pick and more important that you consciously practice focusing on just that one thing.

Technology is a constant distractor from being present, as that little "bing" or "beep" can pull your attention away in an instant. When you are doing a mindfulness task, turn your phone or computer on silent or airplane mode so your focus is not pulled away.

You can also set aside a specific time, perhaps five to ten minutes a day, for your family to practice mindfulness together. It doesn't necessarily have to be everyone sitting down for a group meditation. On the commute to school, you could play "I spy" to focus your attention on the surroundings outside. You might take a mindful walk together each evening, pausing to take in the sounds, smells, and sights of the walk. You can practice mindful eating by taking some time to focus on the smells, sights, and tastes of the meal you are eating together. Or, right before bedtime, you can pause to do some relaxing breathing together, play a short recording of guided imagery activity (e.g. someone reading a script describing a calm place), or progressively relax certain parts of your body.

Mindful Parenting: Mindfulness Benefits for the Whole Family

Mindful parents create mindful children. Ever hear the adage "Monkey see, monkey do"? Children learn by watching, and they learn negative behaviors as easily as positive ones. For example, if your child observes you constantly being distracted by your phone or technology, he begins to think that constant distraction is the norm. If you give your full attention when doing a task or interacting with someone, your child will be more likely to do the same. Point out when you are being fully present by saying out loud, "I am putting my phone away so I can put my full attention into this activity." Being explicit about your mindfulness practice can help your child learn the tools.

Another reason you need to take up this practice is because you can only be there for your kids if you take care of yourself. It is tempting as a parent to neglect yourself, focusing entirely on your kids and forgetting about your own (or your partner's) needs. This is a huge mistake. Not only is it completely impossible—no matter how hard you push yourself you still need to sleep and eat, among other things—it sets a terrible example for your children. Remember, children learn most from what they see you do. If you do not model healthy self-care, how can they possibly learn it for themselves?

CORE PRACTICE

Think of a core practice as a daily habit of the mind. A core practice is a habit you commit to doing on a regular basis. While you may not have time to sit and meditate for an hour each day, there are other core practices that can fit your lifestyle. There are many different kinds of core practices, and each one is useful in different ways and for different people. No single core practice is better than another; they all lead to the same destination, which is the ability to be consciously present in this moment.

Ultimately, your core practice should be something that takes your focus away from fixating on thoughts or feelings and brings you back to your body and the present moment. Try out the following practices, and find the one that works best for you.

Meditation practices usually involve some awareness of the breath. Breath is the strongest bridge between your body and mind, and when the mind gets carried away the breath can help bring you back to the present reality.

To demonstrate how breath is a bridge between body and mind, consider this: Hyperventilating can give you a panic attack. Breathing evenly and deeply increases oxygen flow throughout your body, which helps you calm down, slow your heartbeat, and relax. Breath is a major point of leverage between your body and mind. Although you cannot force your mind to get rid of a thought or emotion, what you can do is intentionally set your mind's direction and pace. Breathing is one very effective way of doing so.

There are many ways to practice with your breath. Traditional Zen meditation begins with the instruction to count the breath in cycles of ten:

Inhale, one; exhale, one.

Inhale, two; exhale, two.

And so on.

When you lose count or notice that a thought has arisen and distracted you from counting your breath, notice the thought that took you away from your counting, acknowledge it, exhale, and begin again from zero. Should you actually make it all the way to ten without losing your focus, which is really more difficult than it sounds, just return to zero and continue.

Particularly for beginners, this is very helpful because it gives you something to do (counting) that is connected to a physical experience you can control (the breath), and gives you an easy way to check yourself when you start to drift. Be aware, you will certainly drift . . . everyone does. That's part of why it is called a practice.

Losing count in breath practice is not a mistake. Actually, you should think of it as a success. This is entirely the point of the practice: to notice when your mind drifts off, acknowledge what thought or feeling caused the drift, and consciously return to the present moment. Instead of thinking, "Oops, there I go again" when you lose count, say to yourself "Got one!" and keep it up.

You can carry this breath counting throughout many activities in your day. As you become more seasoned in counting your breath (you'll know because you routinely get to "ten" without drifting off into other thoughts), you can start counting only on the exhalation:

Inhale, exhale, "one."

Inhale, exhale, "two."

MANTRA

Many practitioners of mindfulness find it helpful to use a mantra, which is a simple phrase you repeat to yourself over and over again to help guide your attention. The mantra can be anything at all that works for you: an affirmation, a reminder, words of encouragement, or something totally meaningless.

James Ford, a contemporary American Zen teacher, is fond of saying "Just" on the inhalation, and "This" on the exhalation. The Korean Zen teacher Seung Sahn taught students to think "Clear mind, clear mind, clear mind" on the inhale, and "Don't know . . . " very slowly on the exhale. One monk even taught the mantra "Coca-Cola." "Om" is another popular mantra. It really doesn't matter what mantra you use. If it helps you connect your awareness to the present moment, it is a useful mantra.

If you are a more kinesthetic person, you may find it useful to focus on your body as you practice. This can be particularly helpful if you find yourself physically restless or fidgety when you try to meditate. Some people just need to move! The key idea is to work with yourself as you naturally are, not to force yourself to do something awkward and uncomfortable. Mindfulness is about acceptance.

One traditional form of body awareness is to focus your attention on the tip of your nose and cultivate an awareness of the physical sensation of breathing. You can attune to the rhythm of your breath, the cool sensation of the inhale and the warm sensation of the exhale. You can try this in combination with counting or with a mantra, whatever you find works best for you.

Awareness of the contact between your feet and the ground is a powerful practice to use while walking. Whether you are just walking from one room to another, going out for a stroll, going for a run, or working out at the gym, awareness of the contact between your feet and the ground can help you be more present. This can help prevent the mind from wandering off at times when it can be very tempting to do so.

Another powerful way to practice with the body is to focus your awareness on the soles of your feet and the sensation of the contact between your feet and the ground. This can be a very anchoring practice as it helps the body maintain a sense of itself in connection with the earth. As you become more aware of where you are in space, the mind naturally calms and becomes more centered, as if gravity were affecting your thoughts as well as your body.

WORKING WITH THOUGHTS AND EMOTIONS

The human brain is built to think and feel. Thoughts and feelings happen whether you want them to or not, and this is completely natural. Sometimes it can be exciting and other times quite stressful. If the thought or feeling is one you really don't want to have, it is all the more difficult to work with.

What you need to keep in mind is that thoughts are a natural product of the brain. People tend to regard their thoughts and emotions as important and meaningful in some way, as if they were somehow indicative of one's character. Ultimately, it isn't your thoughts that determine the kind of person you are, it is what you *do* that really matters.

When you look closely at how thoughts arise in your mind, you will notice that there are really two types. Some thoughts come about as the result of a deliberate action on your part. These are the thoughts you have when you are consciously thinking about something or trying to solve a problem. Other thoughts come about in a way that is more passive: An idea comes up and you begin to ruminate on it. This in turn leads to a series of other thoughts that can go on and on. Thinking in this way is like riding a wild horse: You end up hanging on and going wherever the horse takes you. This kind of thinking can often lead to distraction and feelings of stress, anxiety, and fear. The difference between the two types of thinking is intention, and bringing intention to your thoughts is what mindfulness is all about.

Unfortunately, most schools do not teach students how to manage their thoughts. People are generally at the mercy of their minds, subject to the whims of their thoughts and emotions, believing them to be in some way a true and accurate reflection of reality. This is not actually the case. Thoughts are thoughts, nothing more. To be sure, thoughts come in many flavors; some are pleasant, others are not so pleasant, and can even be frightening or downright disturbing. Mindfulness practice gives you a set of tools to work with all of your thoughts constructively, and can help modulate their impact on both you and those around you.

WORKING WITH EMOTIONS

Emotions shape your interpretation and understanding of the world. They are in some ways analogous to wearing different colored sunglasses. When you put on the blue pair, everything appears to be blue; when you put on the yellow pair, everything appears to be tinted yellow. In a similar way, your emotions change what you experience and how you respond (or react) to these experiences. When you are mindful of your emotions, you can recognize the "color of sunglasses" you are wearing at any given moment and perhaps even have an opportunity to take them off.

Imagine being awake all night with a sick child. In the morning, you have a nasty argument with your partner about cleaning up last night's dishes, and leave for work in an awful mood. You're exhausted, angry, and stressed out. To beat the Dunkin' Donuts drive-through line, you park and go inside. To your dismay a family with three kids is in line in front of you. The children are laughing loudly, and now you're angry with the parents for not making their children be quiet. It also seems like they are purposely taking forever to order. Time seems to slow down, and now you worry about being late for work. For some reason, all you want to do is scream and push that stupid happy family out of your way.

The expression "seeing red" is very fitting here. Emotions are the foundations of human experience. When you are swept away by feelings of frustration and stress, anything around you can fuel the fire of these emotions. When you're angry, you're at odds with whatever environment you are in; you can use anything as an excuse to remain angry or to escalate the intensity. Once you get to this point, it is very difficult to rein yourself in.

This same "colored sunglasses" phenomenon is true of any emotion, including joy. For example, imagine that you're about to go on a trip to see your best friend. You stayed up most of the night packing and preparing the house so your spouse can handle the kids alone. Despite the exhaustion, you can't help but be excited. On your way to the airport you stop at a Dunkin' Donuts for coffee and go inside. Just as in the previous example, a family with three children is in line in front of you. The kids are laughing loudly; watching the way they play with each other reminds you of your own children, and you can't help but smile. It takes some time for the family to get their order in, which you completely understand—you know that ordering breakfast with three happy, hyper kids at your feet can be like trying to herd kittens. You glance at your watch, and see there is plenty of time to get to the airport. *What a sweet family*, you might think.

The issue is not about what thoughts come into your head. All sorts of ideas and emotions will arise for you as a parent, and many of them will not be helpful or pleasant. The question is, how do you handle them as they come up?

Mindfulness is a powerful tool for working with your emotions, and the first step is simply noticing what feelings come up under different circumstances. When you notice that you are getting frustrated, for example, this is an opportunity. Paying attention to the feeling as it arises means that you are not blindly swept away by the feeling. This moment of awareness gives you more control over what you say and do.

WORKING WITH THOUGHTS

You cannot ultimately control your thoughts. Thoughts come up no matter what, and often follow habitual paths in the brain that form over the course of a person's life. People have thoughts about the future, memories from the past, innovative ideas, small observations, violent fantasies, questions about existence—the range of human thought is incredible.

It's not merely the ability to think, reason, remember, and plan that sets our species apart. The fact that we can influence our minds in real time makes human beings truly unique. When a person chooses not to exercise that influence, his thoughts run amok.

Thoughts have no substance unto themselves. They can make you feel things that are very real, and they may inspire action of some kind, but a thought itself is like a puff of smoke: here one moment and gone the next, leaving no trace except your memory of it. Thoughts exist only within your mind, and though some thoughts may recur, they are not permanent.

The goal of mindfulness is not to stop thoughts and emotions from coming up; mindfulness is about paying attention to the thoughts and emotions that come up, without being completely swept away by them.

Important Points to Consider

Being mindful isn't always easy. Sometimes you may drift off course, but with practice and patience, soon it will become part of your daily routine. When in doubt, remember these benefits:

1. When you bring mindfulness to your parenting, not only do you become more of the parent you want to be, but your child will learn from your behavior.

2. The very core of mindfulness practice is to pay attention to whatever arises, moment to moment. This is incredibly useful when it comes to parenting a child with ADHD, since often parents will be more aware of the negative moments, and forget to focus on the positive moments.

3. When you practice paying attention, you will notice many things both in your mind and in the world around you that you may not have noticed before. This can also transfer to your relationship with your child. The more mindful you are as a parent, the more you learn about your child.

4. By practicing mindfulness with your child, you are teaching her to be aware of her emotions, which can help give her space to choose how she wants to react to a situation.

5. Mindfulness has a positive impact on preventing anxiety and depression.

6. Practicing mindfulness with your child can be as easy as playing "I Spy" when you are driving her to school. Simplicity is key.

 **CHAPTER 9**

Helping Your Child Succeed at School

Because children with ADHD symptoms have so much trouble in traditional classrooms, many mentally withdraw early on and drop out at the first opportunity. This is unfortunate, because some simple classroom changes, special education help, or a change in schools can make for a happy and successful educational career. First, it is important that you and your child's educators are on the same page regarding his ADHD diagnosis. You want to have an open dialogue with his teachers and principal before any issues arise. Let them know what your concerns are, and together brainstorm ways to help your child. They may even have suggestions on how you can help your child succeed outside of the classroom.

Public or Private School?

When looking for the best school for your child with ADHD, don't get too concerned with whether the school is public or private, and focus instead on the merits and drawbacks of each school. Both public and private schools have pluses and minuses when it comes to educating children with ADHD.

THE PROS OF PUBLIC SCHOOLS

A public school may be the best resource for you and your child for a variety of reasons. For starters, public schools are free. Some private schools can cost as much or more than college. Your child doesn't have to pass admissions tests and interviews to get in—another factor to consider, given that many children with ADHD may not test well, even if they have high IQs.

Your child's homework load will probably be lighter if he goes to public school, and he can't be forced out if his grades suffer.

THE PROS OF GOING PRIVATE

In general, private schools offer smaller class sizes and a higher student-to-teacher ratio, which makes it more likely that your child will get the attention he needs. Your child won't be forced to attend a specific public school, but is free to attend any private school in the country, or even in the world.

If your child has a very high IQ and gets bored easily, he may benefit from a private school with an academically challenging, rigorous, and personalized academic program.

Most private schools also rely less on testing than public schools and more on a variety of factors to determine student achievement. Some do away with grades altogether and use a "pass–fail" or narrative report system.

Many schools, both public and private, are integrating mindfulness into the curriculum. When considering the best school for your child, ask the administration if they have mindfulness programs or if their staff has had training in teaching mindfulness to children.

How to Help Your Child Get the Support She Needs at School

By becoming your child's most powerful ally and advocate, you can help ensure she gets the help and support she needs at school. Learn everything you can about ADHD, as well as your child's educational and legal rights so you can more effectively work with school personnel. It's never too late to start educating yourself, building bridges with school personnel, and keeping detailed records.

There are many excellent resources for parents of children with ADHD, including books, medical studies, and organizations. Be sure you understand everything about your child's condition, symptoms, and method of treatment. Ask your child's physician about the most up-to-date information on ADHD. Also ask him to explain behavior that may interfere with your child's ability to learn or function at school and suggest ways you can effectively control problems.

Turning Teachers and Administrators Into Allies

As a parent, it's essential to build bridges with teachers and other school personnel to ensure your child is getting the help and attention he needs. Most children with ADHD can succeed in a regular classroom, but sometimes children need additional assistance or adjustments.

If you feel your child is not getting the attention he needs in class, do not immediately blame the teacher. Instead of starting an argument with your child's teacher, approach the topic calmly. This will be better for everyone involved.

Make sure your child's teacher has the necessary training and experience to deal with your child. Remember that many teachers are already handicapped with too many students, and not enough assistance and materials. If you feel your child's teacher isn't equipped to deal with ADHD, talk to the teacher about ways you can collaborate with her, or ask the school principal if your child can be placed in a different classroom.

TIPS FOR BUILDING BRIDGES WITH TEACHERS

Here are some tips and strategies to build a good communication line with your child's teacher(s):

O Reach out to your child's teacher. Before the school year starts, schedule a get-to-know-you meeting so you can get a better handle on the teacher's teaching and discipline style and determine her experience level in working with children with ADHD. You may also want to use this meeting to provide the teacher with information about your child's symptoms, behavior, and specific learning and academic strengths and weaknesses.

O Develop a school plan with the teacher that capitalizes on your child's strengths and helps overcome his weaknesses. Look at constructive ways to deal with behavior problems that may be related to ADHD. This plan is a work in progress that will change as your child gets older and progresses through the school system.

O Don't be afraid to ask for special help for your child, whether it's tutoring or special assistance with homework, study, or organizational skills. Some school districts have tutors and other local resources that can help your child bridge academic gaps.

O Maintain an open line of communication with your child's teacher so you can work together to resolve any new or ongoing problems. Keep the teacher abreast of any changes in symptoms, treatments, or medication changes that may have an impact on schoolwork.

O Show your interest by visiting the classroom and volunteering for activities and projects.

O Ask your child's teacher to give you regular progress reports on your child's classroom performance, homework assignments, discipline issues, etc.

○ Schedule an end-of-school conference with your child's teacher to review your child's progress and look at ways to improve performance in the year ahead. You may also want to ask about teachers your child may have in the upcoming year and how you can best help your child succeed in school.

○ Keep your child in the loop. Make sure he understands that you support his teacher, and outline how you expect him to behave and perform in the classroom setting. You may also want to tell your child how he will be disciplined in the event he misbehaves, and what he may earn if he follows school rules.

○ Maintain all treatment regimens provided by your physician, including medication, behavior modification, and other modalities to help control ADHD symptoms at school and at home.

○ Develop consistency between school and home by using the same language and signals used by your child's teacher to indicate inappropriate behavior and to reward exceptional performance.

○ Help your child get organized by using lists and calendars to keep track of tests, homework assignments, and projects. Show older children how to use computers and assistive technology to facilitate learning. Teach them how to take good notes and show them how to highlight or annotate information to make essential points stand out.

BUILDING BRIDGES WITH SCHOOL PERSONNEL

As well as developing a good line of communication with your child's teachers, you should also get to know other school personnel who will have an impact on your child's learning environment, including the school principal and special education teachers.

THE IMPORTANCE OF KEEPING GOOD RECORDS

When you have a child with ADHD, keeping good records can make or break your child's academic success. Good records can help you monitor your child's academic and behavior progress and help identify academic patterns that may signal the need for adjustments in medication or treatment.

Make sure you keep and continually update the following forms and records:

○ ADHD evaluations used to evaluate what type of ADHD your child has, to help determine the best course of treatment

○ Evaluations for coexisting medical conditions with similar symptoms

○ History of medications to keep track of all medications your child has taken and is currently taking to treat ADHD

○ School progress records, including school plans, progress reports from the teacher, grades, end-of-year reports, and standardized testing results

○ Individualized Education Program (If your child is in special education and has an IEP, keep a copy on file so you have it handy in case other health professionals treating your child need to see it.)

When Your Child with ADHD Has Special Needs

If achievement tests indicate that your child is not progressing as expected based on her IQ test score, she may be diagnosed with a learning disability. Special education can help, but so may a better mainstream classroom environment.

Make sure the teacher of your special education child with ADHD is incorporating the following principles into her regular instruction:

○ Intellectual challenges geared to the student's skill level. Lessons that are too easy or too boring won't hold students' attention, whereas lessons that are too hard cause undue frustration and cause students to give up.

○ Emphasis on understanding and applying concepts. Most teachers place too much emphasis on acquiring information through rote memorization, which many students perceive as useless and tend to forget soon after they are tested on it.

○ Involvement in setting learning objectives. Some students benefit more from the opportunity to learn a little about many subjects; some do better exploring a single subject in depth.

○ Opportunities to pursue individual interests. Students are more motivated when they choose the topic they want to learn about. Virtually any topic can be investigated from the standpoint of any school subject.

○ Self-paced learning. Some students need more time to learn the material. They just do. That is not a reflection of how intelligent they are.

Taking Advantage of Special Services

If your child has a learning disability or special needs, special education help may be a good option. Special education services may involve going to a special classroom all day, getting extra help in a particular subject for an hour a week, or anything in between. It may mean having a specially trained teacher come to the regular classroom to work with your child. The first step in seeing if your child requires special services to make adequate educational progress is to ask her school for a team meeting to discuss additional supports that can be put into place. Review these supports a month or so later to see if they were sufficient. If interventions in the general education classroom are not sufficient, you can submit a written request for an evaluation. You may wish to send the request via certified mail to the school or the district office that handles special services.

DOES MY CHILD QUALIFY?

To qualify for special education, a child's ADHD symptoms must cause significant learning or behavior problems at school. Only the school can determine if a child qualifies, but parent input and additional data from your child's physician, psychologist, or health-care professional can build support for your case for eligibility. The Individuals with Disabilities Education Improvement Act (IDEIA) legally obligates public schools to ensure that children with disabilities have equal access to a free and appropriate education. Although ADHD does not have an eligibility category in and of itself, it falls under the category "Other Health Impairment," which includes children who have "limited strength, vitality, or alertness, including a heightened alertness to environmental stimuli, that results in limited alertness with respect to the educational environment," that "adversely affects a child's educational performance."

SECTION 504

Sometimes students do not need the full range of special education services, but rather formal accommodations to their program in the general education setting. For these students, a "504 Plan" may be sufficient. The 504 Plan essentially formalizes all the accommodations and modifications to your child's schooling (e.g. extra time on tests, extra breaks, flexible deadlines, etc.). To qualify to receive services under Section 504, a student must have a disability that "substantially limits one or more major life functions, including education, learning, and behavior." ADHD falls into this category. Students must receive "appropriate accommodations and modifications" to the regular classroom that are tailored to their individual needs. You can request a 504 evaluation at any time—before, concurrently, or after a special education evaluation. Your child's needs should drive the referral—if you think accommodations alone are sufficient, request a 504 meeting. If you think your child needs more specialized support, perhaps with a case manager or specialized teacher, request an evaluation for special education.

It is a good idea to request a copy of your school district's policies and procedures for complying with IDEIA and Section 504. It will list your rights and the district's responsibilities. If your complaints are not satisfied, you can call the Office for Civil Rights hotline of the U.S. Department of Education at (800) 421-3481 for information about how to proceed.

Mentoring Children with ADHD

Studies show that strong and supportive mentoring relationships between adults and children who have ADHD help children do better in school, and improve their self-image and school attendance.

For a mentorship to work, a child should be matched with an adult mentor who has similar personal traits. In some schools, children with ADHD are matched with college students with ADHD who are having similar ADHD learning challenges. Other mentor programs may match a child with ADHD who has an interest in a specific career with an adult in that career.

Eye to Eye is a national mentoring and advocacy program for students with ADHD that matches young students with high school or college students who also have ADHD. Tutors help children with learning challenges, help them develop special gifts, and work with teachers to develop customized materials for students with ADHD. For more information, visit *http:// eyetoeyenational.org.*

Should Your Child Tell His Friends He Has ADHD?

Many children with ADHD—and even their parents—struggle with whether to tell friends they have the disorder. Some believe it is better that friends understand what they are going through so they can be more understanding and flexible when ADHD symptoms flare up. Others worry that telling friends they have ADHD will scare them away or cause friends to start treating them with kid gloves.

According to experts, there's really no one answer. In many cases, the right decision may be based on the severity of your child's symptoms, and/ or the closeness of the particular friendship.

If your child's symptoms are mild and he's able to manage or disguise most of them with medication and therapy, there may be no reason to tell friends or even teachers he has ADHD, unless you and your child feel that telling them would strengthen his friendships and relationships with them.

On the other hand, if your child's symptoms are more severe and/or frequently disrupt her life and the lives of others, telling friends and teachers she has the condition is probably essential. It will help friends be more understanding, forgiving, and flexible when your child's symptoms flare, and it will ensure your child receives the special services and accommodations she requires in the classroom setting.

Should I Get Involved at My Child's School?

Studies show that children with ADHD get better grades and have better relationships with classmates and teachers when their parents are involved in their schools. This is particularly true if your child is in elementary school or middle school. However, you may want to take a cautious approach if your teen is in high school, as children in this age group are more interested in carving out their own identities than bonding with parents.

Some productive ways to offer your services include coaching a sports team, chairing a special hobby club, assisting your child's teacher with a special class, chaperoning a school dance or field trip, or attending PTA meetings and activities as well as parent-teacher meetings. If your teenager with ADHD is on a sports team, she may prefer you show your support by cheering her on at games.

Important Points to Consider

For some children with ADHD, school can be a challenge. As a conscious parent, there are certain things you can do to help your child succeed in school, such as:

1. Open a line of communication with your child's teachers and principal. Being able to speak candidly about your child's progress and struggles can help ensure success.

2. Do research on which school is best for your child. Some schools now even incorporate mindfulness programs into their daily curriculum.

3. If you find yourself at odds with a teacher, stay calm and look for a peaceful solution. Model positive conflict-resolution for your child. Creating an "us versus them" mentality with school staff can be destructive for your child's relationship and willingness to work with his teacher.

4. Get involved as much as possible in your child's education by visiting the classroom and talking with the teacher.

5. Being organized is just as important for you as for your child. Keep paperwork and evaluations of your child's progress neatly put away in a safe place.

CHAPTER 10

Coping with Social Challenges

As a member of society, your child with ADHD is expected to interact and communicate with others on a regular basis. She needs to be capable of understanding what friends and teachers say, and to read and interpret nonverbal cues so she can behave appropriately in social settings. Unfortunately, many children with ADHD can't follow conversations, stay focused on lengthy discussions, or read body language—and they may respond to conversations or social interactions in ways that are not appropriate, consistent, or relevant. Discussing appropriate behaviors and practicing mindfulness techniques can help your child improve social interaction skills and encourage positive experiences with peers.

Why Making Friends Is More Difficult for Children with ADHD

Friends are important for youngsters' mental and physical well-being. Stress born of social isolation and peer conflict suppresses the immune system and increases vulnerability to illness and depression.

For your child to master the art of getting along with others, making friends, and maintaining healthy relationships, you will need to teach a number of essential social skills.

Unfortunately, many children with ADHD symptoms have poor social skills because they do not tune in to the subtleties of social interactions or they misread social cues. They can benefit from reminders to pay attention, and they can often be more objective than other children when watching how peers interact with one another.

MINDFULNESS PRACTICES FOR UNDERSTANDING SOCIAL SITUATIONS

Mindfulness activities, such as making observations of a social scene, may help your child. Have your child imagine she is in a helicopter circling over a social situation in which she is present. Ask her to take in all the information about how people are acting and interacting. Is she fitting in? For example, if all the children are seated at their desks, quietly working, is she sharpening her pencil? If all the children at the birthday party are playing a game together, is she on the other side of the room? This technique for looking at the "big picture" may help boost her social awareness.

IMPORTANCE OF MATURITY LEVEL

For children to get along with one another, maturity level is more important than age. If your youngster's social skills are very poor, she may have fewer conflicts and more in common with younger children.

Older children tend to make allowances for younger ones, therefore they are often more tolerant of immature behavior. Hence, your child may do better with playmates that are younger or older than with kids her own age.

To help your child make friends at school, you might have the teacher ask a classmate to mentor your child and provide tips for getting along with others. Research indicates that simply having a well-liked student and an unpopular one do a project together provides an enduring social connection.

ADHD Symptoms that Flare in Social Settings

Social situations can be difficult for children with ADHD. Because they feel less confident and more stressed out in social settings than other children, they often experience a flare of ADHD symptoms. Praising your child when she has successful social interactions is a great way to boost her confidence.

Even if your child has become adept at making and keeping friends, a particularly stressful social situation is likely to trigger:

O Feeling like he doesn't fit in

O Having trouble following conversations

O Having trouble tuning out extraneous noises or music

O Feeling overwhelmed at the slightest thing

O Feeling the need to dominate a conversation

O Blurting out confidential, inappropriate, or irrelevant information during conversations

O Being unable to read and translate body language, voice tone, facial expressions, or simple nuances of interaction

O Reacting in an overemotional, defensive, or overly intense way

O Jumping to the wrong conclusions

- Feeling defensive

- Feeling that others are always criticizing and blaming him

- Being reluctant to contribute or participate in a conversation for fear of embarrassing himself

- Being viewed by others as standoffish, disinterested, snobbish, or bored

Remind your child that using mindfulness techniques to calm herself when she is in a stressful situation can be very helpful. Sometimes just taking a few deep breaths or a few quiet minutes away from the crowd can do the trick.

Helping Your Child Deal with Anger and Criticism

Children with ADHD are criticized, rejected, and teased so often that they can become defensive and angry when others criticize them. Many children with ADHD also have very short tempers and explosive mood swings that may erupt without warning in social settings, causing them social embarrassment.

HOW TO HELP YOUR CHILD KEEP HER COOL

Practice with your child so she learns how to control her temper. Here are some helpful strategies you can role-play together. Mindfulness is key for many of these strategies.

- Encourage your child to count to ten before reacting or responding to an unkind comment.

- Encourage your child to stick up for herself and to ask someone to clarify or explain if she thinks another person's comment was untrue or unfair.

- Teach your child to use exercise to work off her anger. Taking a quick walk around the block can help your child chill out.

- Practice clever comebacks with your child to things she gets teased about frequently.

- Teach your young child mindfulness activities that involve deep breathing to combat anger, such as blowing up balloons, blowing bubbles or pinwheels, or doing deep belly breathing with a toy on his belly so he can see it moving up and down.

- Model for your child how to deal with anger by doing your own calming strategy and then pointing it out to her so she can see how it helped you calm down.

ACCEPTING CONSTRUCTIVE CRITICISM

Children with ADHD are often criticized and rejected and may not be able to distinguish valid, helpful criticism from nasty teasing and bullying. Encourage your child to consider the source when deciding how to respond to criticism. If it comes from a classmate who is usually a bully, your child can probably ignore it. If it comes from a well-meaning teacher or school principal, your child will probably want to listen carefully and heed the advice.

Dealing with Impatience

Whether it's butting into conversations without being invited, becoming frustrated for not getting something right, or refusing to wait their turn, children with ADHD are notoriously impatient with others and themselves—a trait that often rears its ugly head in social situations.

Before your child jumps into a conversation, encourage him to listen for several minutes to make sure he fully understands what is being discussed. Before responding, encourage him to collect his thoughts, quiet his mind, and think about what he could say that would add to the conversation.

The mindfulness practice of deep, purposeful, and diaphragmatic breathing is an excellent way to teach patience. When one is deep breathing, it is near impossible to blurt something out! If your child can identify feelings and situations where she is more likely to blurt out and take a few deep breaths when she is in that situation, she can become more patient and thoughtful in thinking through if what she wants to say is appropriate. You might model this for your child when you are feeling impatient, such as when you are in a long line, by taking some purposeful deep breaths and noting for your child that you are doing so in order to keep calm.

Teaching Your Child How to Share and Compromise

Sharing and compromising can be hard for children with low self-esteem, so lots of children with ADHD symptoms need help in this area. Youngsters who are constantly on the defensive commonly fear that if they give an inch, they will end up having everything taken from them.

Explain the miracle of sharing. By giving a friend a gift, your child stands to keep a friend. At the same time, it is not possible to buy friends. She must be able to give without expecting anything in return. The point of compromising is to create a win/win situation. If your child and a friend cannot agree, she needs to toss out some suggestions that she thinks both of them might feel okay about.

> Role-play and/or give your child examples: "If you want to play one video game and your friend wants to play a different one, offer to play his game for ten minutes if he will then play yours for ten minutes."

Direct your child to give positive feedback to her friends by letting them know something that she likes or appreciates about them. She can tell a classmate that she liked her oral report, compliment her on her new haircut, or say something positive about her expertise at jump rope, long division, or anything else. She, of course, needs to be sincere and to keep her comments simple.

Very needy children make peers uncomfortable by piling on the praise, so stress the importance of confining herself to one positive comment per day. Model this important social behavior by giving your child positive feedback, but aim for one positive comment per hour when interacting with your youngster.

Helping Your Child Make Friends

Research shows that people who have lots of friends not only live longer, but also get sick less often than people with few or no friends. Unfortunately, children with ADHD may find that making and keeping friends takes more energy and focus than finishing their schoolwork. Fortunately, you can teach them many essential skills for making and keeping friends and role-play at home until appropriate behavior and responses become second nature.

To help a young child learn to initiate friendships, you may need to take him by the hand and walk him over to meet another child, introduce them, and suggest they play together.

Here are some other ways to help your child develop and keep friendships:

○ Teach a child by giving him a mini-lesson en route to a social gathering. On the way to his first soccer practice, instruct him to say, "Hi, my name is Jim. What's yours?" Give him a conversation opener, too. "This is my first time playing soccer. How about you?"

○ If your child thinks your suggestions are "dumb," tell him to watch to see how other people start conversations and report back to you. Afterward, ask him what he noticed. The best way to learn social skills is to watch how other people interact.

○ Many children with ADHD symptoms have poor social skills because they do not tune in to the subtleties of social interactions or they misread social cues. They benefit from reminders to pay attention, and they can often be more objective when watching how peers interact with one another.

○ An adolescent may pretend that your recommendations are too old-fashioned to be of use. Nevertheless, your teen may refashion your ideas to fit his social group's slang and use them. When he's leaving for a dance, you might suggest, "Go up to someone you recognize, and say, 'Hi. Aren't you in Dr. Bob's third period English class?' or whatever. Whether or not you are right, you can start a conversation about your English teacher by asking how she likes her class."

Helping Your Child Tune in to Nonverbal Cues

Although your child can't "fix" many symptoms of childhood ADHD caused by the neurobiological imbalance in her brain, there are many tips and strategies she can role-play with you to learn appropriate behavior and rein in out-of-control ADHD behavior.

Role-play so your child learns to listen carefully to conversations and respond to playful comments with playful answers, and to serious questions with serious answers.

REHEARSING LIKELY SCENARIOS

One way to make sure your child doesn't blurt out the wrong thing is to have her rehearse appropriate responses to a variety of scenarios that are likely to occur. Before she goes to a party, she might rehearse responses to questions that typically arise in casual party chat, such as, "How do you like your teachers?" or "How is your baseball team doing this year?" Have your child practice responses with you in various fictional settings until she feels comfortable.

By rehearsing appropriate responses with you, your child will also learn to better distinguish between appropriate and inappropriate responses. This will alleviate her anxiety in social settings as well as give her an arsenal of appropriate rehearsed responses to draw on in real-life settings.

LEARNING NOT TO HOG THE CONVERSATION

Because they have trouble reading nonverbal cues, many children with ADHD have a tendency to dominate conversations or keep talking long after everyone has lost interest.

Role-play being in a group conversation, and encourage your child to listen far more than she talks and keep her comments short. Show her how to be kind and honest without being insincere or overly blunt, to be careful about jumping into conversations before she's invited, and to limit her comments to the topic at hand rather than dominating the conversation with irrelevant or unrelated matters.

You can also point out socially appropriate behavior and social faux pas in books, television shows, videos, stories, or movies. When appropriate, you can stop and ask questions such as, "What is that child doing that is positive/negative?" "How might the other child be feeling?" or "What do you think will happen next?" to get your child to start thinking about how particular actions have effects on social dynamics. Then, reference the lesson when your child experiences a similar problem ("Remember when Daniel Tiger waited his turn and made his friend happy?" "Remember in that movie when the girl posted something online without thinking it through and created a huge problem at her school?"). This will help him think through positive ways to interact in social situations.

Benefits of Role-Playing

Role-playing with your child is an excellent way to help him rehearse and practice appropriate social behavior and talk so he feels more confident and relaxed in social settings.

Many children with ADHD become nervous and flabbergasted when they go to parties or other social settings. They often embarrass themselves by exhibiting ADHD behavior such as butting in, dominating the conversation, yammering on and on when no one is interested, saying rude or overly blunt things to others, or saying inappropriate or "clueless" things in conversations.

Why is role-playing so important for ADHD kids? Role-playing gives your child a safe place to practice appropriate social behavior until he gets it right, so he doesn't blurt out things that cause him to be ostracized, shunned, or ignored by classmates. Role-play with your child before he goes to a party to rehearse small talk and clever responses.

THE ART OF SMALL TALK

Role-play with your teen so he feels comfortable with the art of small talk. Tell him he just wants to skim off the basics, and remind him that when it comes to small talk, it's better to know a little about a lot of different things than a lot about just one thing.

Another easy way your teen with ADHD can facilitate small talk is to read up on sports and local and international news, or see what is trending in social media before going to a party so he has lots of easy conversation starters at his disposal.

REHEARSE BOWING OUT BEFORE BLOWING OUT

If your child finds himself in a small group discussion he can't follow or can't keep up with, tell him not to get so impatient with himself that he goes overboard trying to think up an appropriate response that may not hit the mark. If your child is truly confused and/or bewildered by the train of conversation, or if the topic of conversation is simply over his head, practice helping him find a good excuse to bow out politely before he reaches the point of no return—when his hyperactivity or impulsivity may cause him to butt in or blurt out something that may be inappropriate or irrelevant. "Where's the restroom?" or "I'd better rejoin my friend," or "I think I need a glass of water" are always handy excuses for making a graceful exit.

LIMITING PERSONAL DISCLOSURE

Many children with ADHD let hyperactivity and impulsivity get the best of their tongues and they divulge too much personal information about themselves or they break confidences. Make sure your child understands that divulging too much personal information about herself or gossiping about others makes strangers feel uncomfortable and pressured to reciprocate with personal details about themselves or others.

Tell your child that sharing too much overly positive information about himself with others could have the opposite effect of what he was hoping to achieve. Instead of making people feel closer to him, it could come across as bragging or boasting, and leave some people wondering if he's really telling the truth, or simply exaggerating or lying to try to impress or intimidate them.

WIGGLING OUT OF DIFFICULT SITUATIONS

Teenagers benefit from being given the words they can use in difficult social situations. Before your teen leaves for a party, tell him how to respond to antisocial pressures: "If someone asks if you want a cigarette, you can say, 'No, I don't smoke.' If you need an excuse, you can say, 'I can't, I'm trying out for track,' or 'My parents have noses like beagles and will ground me for life if I come home smelling of smoke.'" Do not bombard your teen with a dozen lectures before he gets together with friends. Tackling one issue per outing is plenty.

Correcting Inappropriate Social Behavior

When you observe your youngster making a social blunder, such as being rude, bossy, selfish, or inconsiderate, be careful about how you intervene. Embarrassing your child in front of her peers almost always does more harm than good. That goes for first graders as well as for teens.

THE IMPORTANCE OF KEEPING IT PRIVATE

To teach your child to be considerate and respectful of peers, you need to demonstrate appropriate behavior. Call your youngster aside and speak with her privately if you need to make a correction. That is also what your youngster needs to do if she is upset with someone. If she criticizes another child in front of a group, she is likely to find herself being shunned or challenged to fight the person she humiliated.

TEACHING WITHOUT PREACHING

Your child will be more willing to heed your advice about social matters if you have a close relationship and if she believes that you understand the social dilemmas she is facing.

An excellent way to achieve a closer relationship and demonstrate that you understand what your child is up against is to share stories from your past. Sharing how you felt about being teased when you were growing up lets your child know that you empathize and have grappled with similar problems.

Telling what you did to try to win friends and influence enemies can give your youngster ideas about new things to try and mistakes to avoid, while helping her to consider her situation more objectively. Recounting personal stories is especially effective with adolescents.

Importance of ADHD Buddies and Support Groups

Instead of trying to weather a social function on his own, suggest that your child ask a close friend to go with him. This buddy can translate conversations your child may have trouble following, as well as interpret nonverbal cues, and give him a friendly nudge or warning look when he starts to dominate the conversation or stray off course.

TESTING THE WATERS

His buddy can also test the waters of small groups at a party by joining the conversation first. If it seems like a friendly group and a conversation your child will be able to participate in successfully, the buddy can wave your child in and introduce him.

SUPPORT GROUPS

ADHD support groups are another place for your child to practice and model appropriate social behavior in a safe, supportive environment. Because everyone in your child's support group has been in a similar dilemma or situation, they can offer strategies to your child that might not have occurred to you.

Helping Your Child Tap Into Social Outlets

Most children with ADHD are unhappy at school and feel unsuccessful a good deal of the time. Finding an activity your child enjoys that helps her feel successful can go a long way to improving the quality of her life. For extracurricular activities to be positive social outlets, your youngster needs to be able to handle herself in a group setting. When choosing activities, your child's interests need to be taken into account.

TWO SIDES OF ORGANIZED SPORTS

When trying to find an extracurricular activity for their children, many parents automatically think about soccer, baseball, and other team sports. They hope that playing a sport will improve coordination and provide good exercise, and that being on a team will instill discipline, teach sportsmanship, and provide a positive social outlet. Some youngsters are very physical, and their happiest times are spent in Little League practices, at hockey tournaments, and playing in volleyball matches.

Are team sports a good idea for my son with ADHD? Maybe, but maybe not. Many children diagnosed with ADHD can be clumsy and inattentive. They are regarded as liabilities by team members and coaches who are more concerned about bringing home a trophy than about having fun. If your child is clumsy, steer him to solo sports such as hiking and cycling.

BENEFITS OF INDIVIDUAL SPORTS

Although team sports are not good choices for many youngsters with ADHD, individual sports are another matter altogether. The emphasis on personal development can lessen the pressure to perform while providing healthful exercise and sensory-motor training. Possibilities include swimming, gymnastics, tennis, aikido, karate, bicycling, skiing, ice-skating, and skateboarding.

Dance is not a sport, but the emphasis on rhythm and body awareness can be good physical therapy for physically awkward youngsters who may not be able to participate in team sports or activities because they lack hand-eye coordination and could be a detriment to teams. Other solo activities your child may enjoy include yoga and tai chi.

TAPPING INTO COMMUNITY CENTERS AND CLUBS

From puppet making to pottery, from judo to jewelry making, from basketball to basket weaving, town parks and recreation departments, youth centers, YMCAs, YWCAs, and many health clubs and fitness centers offer a wealth of fun activities for children.

Open courts at local Ys provide children with the chance to shoot baskets without the pressure to show up for scheduled practices, and to practice without risking spectators catcalling from the bleachers.

During the summer, check to see if your area's Y offers day camps, nature hikes, trips to swimming pools and museums, and other community outings. Youngsters can meet new people without having to worry that their negative reputation at school will interfere. Urge your child to take the opportunity to practice new skills.

If your child is not ready for the intense peer contact of an overnight camp, try a day camp instead. Alternatively, find a camp for children with behavior problems and for at-risk youth at the American Camp Association website at www.acacamps.org. There are many summer camps just for children with ADHD.

MAKING CONNECTIONS AT CHURCHES

Churches and synagogues often have youth groups that are especially kid-friendly. Parents do not have to be members for their children to be welcome. Meetings usually begin and end with a prayer, but the emphasis is on fellowship and fun. Like scouting troops, youth groups sponsored by religious organizations tend to be less structured than school classrooms but more closely supervised than neighborhood free-for-alls. Hence, they can be especially good choices for children with special needs.

If Your Child Is a Loner

Although research shows that loners have more adjustment problems than the social butterflies of the world, that is a group average and is not true for everyone. Some junior technicians would rather build model airplanes, work on the computer, or put together a shortwave radio than trade baseball cards or skateboard with neighbors.

Many youngsters do not want to put time and energy into peers unless they share their interests. Being alone and feeling lonely are very different. It is a mistake to try to cure a child of what does not ail him. If he is happy, that is all that counts. Just be sure that he has not become a loner by default because he has alienated his schoolmates with his inappropriate behavior.

The best solution for a child who is suffering because he lacks friends is to find an activity he likes that he can really get involved in. Like adults, children often bond around shared experiences. Peers with a common interest are more willing to overlook one another's personality quirks. But before searching for ways to fill your child's social calendar, you do need to help your youngster learn some basic social skills.

Important Points to Consider

Making friends is an essential part of development for young people. Here are few things to keep in mind regarding your child's social skills:

1. Age is a factor. It may help your child to become friendly with an older child, as older children tend to be more flexible regarding inappropriate behavior.

2. Your child can use mindfulness techniques such as deep breathing to calm herself when she is in a stressful social situation. Practice calming activities with your child, such as meditation and deep breathing. If she sees you doing it, she'll be more likely to employ the same techniques when she finds herself in a difficult social situation.

3. To boost his confidence, aim to give your child one compliment per hour when you are spending quality time with him.

4. Role-playing can help your child understand different ways to approach his peers. Have your child pretend that you are a new friend and play through an entire interaction together.

5. Keep your corrections private to avoid making a situation worse. If you see your child acting inappropriately, call her aside and let her know how to change her behavior.

CHAPTER 11

Parenting Challenges for Parents of Children with ADHD

Parenting children with ADHD can be a real challenge, regardless of how much you've read up on it or discussed it with other parents. Even when you have the best of intentions, the day-in, day-out grind of dealing with childhood ADHD can exhaust your patience as you try to cope with the condition's effects on your child as well as the entire family. Because ADHD is a genetic condition, you or your spouse may also have it, compounding problems and making good parenting skills even more crucial. Remember that part of being a conscious parent means taking care of yourself. Children often learn by example, so take the time to practice mindfulness exercises and be present as much as possible. Soon your child will be doing the same.

Behavior Strategies for Parents

Trying to raise a child with ADHD can sometimes be overwhelming and confusing. Remember that as the parent, you hold the cards when it comes to helping your child coexist with her symptoms and channel her energy in a constructive way.

If you have ADHD, your parenting can improve when you take care of yourself. A study conducted at the University of Pennsylvania and cited in *Scientific American* (July/August 2015) showed that adults with ADHD improve their parenting skills when they get treated for the disorder—most likely because parents with unresolved medical or mental health issues are more likely to ignore or overreact to kids' misbehavior.

PARENT TRAINING

Parent training is a type of counseling that teaches parents how to work with children who have ADHD to improve the child's behavior and also to improve the parent's relationship with the child. Ask your child's physicians for information about where you can take parent training classes, talk to people in your support group, or contact local universities or the local chapter of CHADD.

Parent training will help you learn to develop limits and boundaries for specific behavior you want to change. It also teaches you to be a more effective disciplinarian by using proactive discipline methods that deal with misbehavior by using time-outs and loss of privileges. You'll also discover ways to reward good behavior and to show your child how she can learn and grow from her mistakes.

PARENT SURVIVAL STRATEGIES

As your child's most important role model and advocate, it's essential that you also stay physically, mentally, and emotionally healthy. If you become overly tired, stressed out, or worn down, you'll have less patience and endurance for dealing with your child's ADHD symptoms. Make sure to follow a healthy diet and exercise program. Find ways to minimize stress, commit to a core mindfulness practice, and get help for illnesses and injuries immediately. Here are other survival tips to try:

○ Take a break. Raising a child with ADHD is an exhausting, time-consuming task. Don't feel guilty about giving yourself some down time, especially if you have ADHD yourself. Head to work early so you can relax over coffee at the local coffee shop; hire a babysitter and go to the movies or out to dinner with your spouse; join a health club and exercise or do yoga at lunchtime or right after work; make time for unwinding with supportive friends.

○ Give yourself a break. Remember that losing your cool and occasionally yelling at your child or losing your patience with her doesn't make you a bad parent. There are many things you can do to help unwind. Practice a guided visualization; whip up a quick breakfast smoothie and be mindful as you drink it; take five to ten minutes to do a mindfulness activity or meditation; read an inspirational eBook, and so on.

○ Don't blame yourself for your child's condition. ADHD is caused by a biochemical imbalance in certain areas of the brain. Although the condition is primarily genetic, it is not caused by bad parenting or a hectic home environment, although these things can worsen symptoms. ADHD is genetic, but it's not your fault if you passed it on to your child.

○ Join a support group. Remember that you don't have to do it all alone. Talk to supportive physicians, therapists, teachers, and parents. Consider joining a support group for parents of children with ADHD where you can exchange information and vent your feelings.

Improving Communication

Miscommunication often runs rampant in families with ADHD. Children with the disorder are often so impatient and impulsive that they don't listen well to what family members are saying and misinterpret things. They also are prone to blurting things out without thinking first, violating confidences, and making rude and hurtful comments.

Improving communication issues in the family may require a therapist's help, although there are also some strategies you can try at home, including:

○ Encourage everyone in the family to become an active listener. This means repeating what someone else says before adding a comment or response of your own.

○ Encourage family members to ask for clarification if they don't understand something. Instead of making assumptions or leaping to the wrong conclusions, encourage everyone to ask what something means.

○ Encourage everyone to avoid criticism. Contrary to the popular phrase, criticism is rarely constructive and usually belittles, angers, or intimidates others. Encourage family members to resist the urge to criticize and remember the age-old maxim, "If you don't have something nice to say, don't say anything at all."

○ Tell family members to preface a negative comment with a positive one. Encourage family members to say something they appreciate about a family member before jumping right into stating what they don't like.

Remind everyone in the family that the path to effective communication is careful listening and understanding what others are saying. Most arguments occur when one person misinterprets or misunderstands what another family member is saying.

Establishing Structure and Setting Rules

Many children with ADHD have no sense of structure or time. Your child is more likely to succeed if you create a home environment that is organized, consistent, and predictable. Build everyday routines and structures to help your child get and stay organized and on time.

HELPING YOUR CHILD STAY FOCUSED

Here are some strategies for helping your child stay organized and focused:

○ Create set routines. Establish a consistent time and place for everything your child does at home, including meals, homework, bedtime, TV time, computer time, play time, etc.

○ Put clocks in several locations around the house, including your child's bedroom. Set timers on clocks, phones, and computers to alert your child that it's time to have dinner, finish his homework, or go to bed.

○ Keep things simple. Many children with ADHD get overwhelmed when they have too many choices. Make sure your child has a few toys or activities to keep him busy, but don't overload him with too much at once or he'll become frustrated.

○ Create a quiet corner. Your child with ADHD needs a quiet place in the home where he can do his homework or read without being distracted or interrupted by other family members.

○ Be a good role model when it comes to being tidy and organized. Your child probably won't understand why he has to tidy his room if the rest of the house is a mess.

○ Keep your children busy after school with structured activities, without overwhelming him with too many choices. Choose an activity that incorporates exercise or mindfulness practice; yoga and tai chi may be good options.

○ Avoid exposing your child to violent TV or video games. These can aggravate or increase hyperactivity and impulsivity.

CREATING REALISTIC RULES AND EXPECTATIONS

Create clear, concise rules for your child with ADHD, and post them in a prominent place in the house so your child can refer to them often. Create clear-cut expectations for how you expect your child to behave, and provide consistent consequences or rewards he values. Keep the rules simple and broad enough that you can reference them easily, such as "Be safe, Be Respectful, and Be Responsible." You can have discussions about specifics as behaviors arise, and add examples for each broad rule. For example, under "Be Responsible" you could add, "Clear your dishes after dinner" or "Put away technology when doing homework."

IMPORTANCE OF PRAISE

Remember that most children with ADHD are used to criticism and rejection, so watch for their good behavior and praise and reward it when you see it to reinforce it—even if it's behavior you'd automatically expect in another child. Rewards can be as simple as a smile and hug, or can take the form of special privileges or gifts.

Improving Organization and Time Management

Many children with ADHD are extremely disorganized, can't prioritize, and lack essential time-management skills. These problems create myriad challenges at school and often cause children with high IQs to fail.

ORGANIZATIONAL STRATEGIES FOR CHILDREN WITH ADHD

Disorganization is a classic symptom of ADHD, and it can make it difficult for your child to do many tasks she needs to do to succeed at school, such as getting projects done on time, prioritizing, breaking up large tasks into small doable pieces, keeping track of books and materials for different classes, and even remembering her class schedule. Here are some strategies you can encourage your child to adopt to get and stay organized in school:

○ Have your child organize projects or tasks on a day calendar and give each task a specific length of time. Don't underestimate. Have her choose a few of the most essential tasks, prioritize them, and then tackle one at a time. If your child tends to forget appointments, set multiple alarms on a computer calendar or cell phone to remind her.

○ Develop a methodical system for big projects. To tackle large or long-term projects, develop a systematic approach. Have your child outline the goal of the project and detail major considerations including interim deadlines. Then have your child break the project down into smaller steps and determine how much time each will take, making sure her estimates are realistic and in line with those short-term deadlines. Tackle one task at a time, and give your child small rewards when each task is completed. Have your child periodically review her timeline to make sure she has enough time to get the project done on time.

○ Remember that organizational strategies may periodically break down, so don't expect perfection. The good news is that once your child has established an organizational technique or experienced an organizational success, it becomes easier to reintroduce it and come up with additional strategies for future projects. Expecting perfect solutions can lead to frustration, recrimination, and loss of self-esteem. Sometimes it's better for your child to accept a less-than-ideal solution and pat herself on the back for the progress she's made.

○ Tune out distractions. If your child usually studies in a busy or noisy environment, it may be difficult for her to focus. If she's distracted by noise or people talking, consider getting headsets or a white noise machine. If she tends to gaze out the window, pull the blinds. Use visual reminders to help her stay alert and focused on tasks. Have her shake off tension and stress that may disrupt her focus by taking a breather on occasion. Have her stretch her arms and legs, shrug her shoulders, scrunch her neck, wiggle her fingers, or take some deep breaths.

TIME-MANAGEMENT SKILLS

To help your child with ADHD get things done on time and manage and organize her time so the most important things get done, encourage her to incorporate these strategies:

○ Create a daily to-do list, either on paper or using technology. To manage the many details of her studies, write every one down, no matter how small or insignificant, and put the list somewhere she'll be able to see it. Advise her to do one at a time.

○ Draw a line through each task as it is completed. She will feel some satisfaction each time she crosses off a task, and she will also see that she is making progress. This reinforcement leads to further progress.

○ Make sure she consults her to-do list throughout the day so she doesn't get sidetracked.

If your child is resistant to a pencil and paper to-do list, apps such as 30/30 and Pomodoro are great ways to set a digital to-do list. Your child can make a plan, set the amount of time she estimates she'll need to spend on it, build in breaks, and see how much time elapsed to keep on track.

BREAKING THE LATENESS HABIT

Whether it's getting a project done on time or getting to work on time, many kids with ADHD struggle with meeting deadlines. One reason is that children with ADHD tend to underestimate how long it actually takes to accomplish something. In addition, their chronic disorganization and clutter prevent them from acting efficiently.

Until your child breaks the lateness habit, encourage her to double or even triple the amount of time she thinks something will take. To become more realistic about how long certain tasks take, have her write down time estimates in her calendar, and then compare them to actual times after she completes the task. This will help her reset her estimation for the next project and include the extra time. The more she records and corrects how long it takes to do something, the better she'll become at narrowing the gap between how long she thinks it will take to accomplish something and how long it actually takes.

It's not impossible for your child to break the lateness habit, but it will take some effort and practice on her part. Encourage her not to fall into the trap of thinking she can finish just one more thing before she leaves. Also encourage her to set multiple alarms to let her know when it's time to leave for school, an important appointment, or a social function.

Using Rewards and Consequences

Psychologists have long recognized that the same straightforward principles and simple procedures work well for animals of all kinds, from human beings to fruit flies. Behavior modification programs are effective for helping children and adults alike eliminate troublesome behaviors, break destructive habits, develop better self-control, and respond in healthier ways. It works by incorporating a system of rewards for positive behavior and consequences or punishments for negative behavior. For more information on the system of rewards and consequences used in behavior modification, see Chapter 14.

Financial Interventions

Parents of children with ADHD often have trouble keeping track of household finances, and no wonder. Many parents also have one or more children with the disorder who are seeing a variety of medical experts, and who may be attending special schools or classes, or receiving specialized assistance in college or in the workplace.

Keeping track of the medical expenses and medications incurred by childhood ADHD is an overwhelming challenge for many parents whose children see one or more specialist for their condition and may take one or more types of medication. Each visit creates a paper trail that needs to be tracked for reimbursement and tax purposes.

The good news is it doesn't take an MBA to set up an easy filing and tracking system for your family. You can do it yourself using these helpful tips:

O Buy an accordion folder for each category of expenses (medical, household, college, summer camp, etc.).

O Label each section of the accordion for specific bills. Include such things as doctor's visits, psychologist's visits, prescription medications, medical insurance, specialized classes for children, disability insurance, legal fees, and transportation and mileage. Every time you get a bill, whether it's a physician's invoice or a credit card slip for a medication, file it in the proper place.

O Remember to keep track of transportation and mileage to and from doctor's visits. Also hold on to receipts for parking, turnpike tolls, gas, and/or mileage, for tax deduction purposes.

O If you'd rather, keep track of your expenses via computer. Quicken Medical Expense Manager is an ideal organizational tool that lets you electronically file in one place insurance information, provider information, exam histories, payments, and disputed claims for each family member. The program also automatically calculates reimbursable mileage, tax deductions, and HSA contributions. Go to *http://quicken-medical-expense-manager.software.informer.com* for more information.

O Consider *www.mint.com,* which also provides free online software for accounting that culls all your bank accounts and credit cards into one program. From there, you can go through each transaction and flag it as a medical expense and create reports at the end of the year for tax purposes.

Support Groups for Parents of Children with ADHD

You already know how and why ADHD can leave your child feeling lonely, isolated, and like a social misfit. One of the easiest and fastest ways to make connections with other parents and children struggling with ADHD is to join a support group in your area.

A support group can provide an avenue where you can make new friends, share your experiences and problems, and gain moral support. Your support group can also keep you informed on the best medical resources in the area as well as special services, disability experts, and colleges and universities that cater to adults with ADHD.

To find a support group near you, check with local colleges, universities, churches and synagogues, community hospitals and clinics, senior citizen centers, or through the local chapter of CHADD, an organization for children and adults with ADHD.

Strategies for Parents

The more you know about childhood ADHD, and the more tools and strategies you have at your disposal, the better you'll be able to manage the various mental, emotional, physical, and lifestyle challenges, setbacks, and detours arising from living with the disorder. Here are ten easy things you can do as a parent to minimize the symptoms of childhood ADHD:

1. Get to the root of things. If your child has been feeling out of sorts or showing signs of depression for two weeks or longer, it's important to get to the bottom of the problem. Children with ADHD can suffer from symptoms of primary or secondary depression, or both. Primary depression is largely inherited and not triggered by life problems such as job loss or relationship problems. Secondary depression usually results from the accumulated frustrations and disappointments of living with undiagnosed or untreated ADHD. Don't be afraid to ask for help if you feel like your child's life is spiraling out of control because of disruptive thoughts or behavior.

2. Find ways to minimize distractions. If your child has ADHD, he already has trouble maintaining focus, and shifting attention to something else when it's necessary. Help your child reduce distractions throughout the day that are likely to derail him, and which may keep him awake all night. To make sure your child isn't distracted by loud music or television when he's trying to study, turn down the volume, turn it off altogether, or have your child use earplugs or white noise machines to block or camouflage the noise. Make sure to create a quiet corner where your child can focus on his homework without being interrupted by other family members.

3. Improve your child's quality of life. Don't assume that having ADHD means your child has to put up with depression and anxiety. If your child is on ADHD medication and still suffers from significant to moderate depression, ask your doctor about prescribing an anti-depressant. Antidepressants boost levels of the neurotransmitters serotonin and norepinephrine, and will help your child maintain feelings of well-being and happiness. Keep in mind however, that antidepressants require extra caution when used by children and adolescents. This is discussed in Chapter 13.

4. Easy does it on carbohydrates and caffeine. Children with ADHD often resort to high-carbohydrate snacks such as candy, chips, or ice cream, or frequent consumption of caffeine, to elevate their moods or increase alertness and energy. The "fix" doesn't last long. Overdoing carbohydrates can lead to weight gain and fatigue, whereas too much caffeine can make your teen feel nervous and jittery and lead to insomnia. To help your child maintain a healthy low-carbohydrate/high-protein, diet, consider creating meals from cookbooks such as The South Beach Diet Cookbook or the Zone diet, both of which have low-carbohydrate meal plans, recipes, and lists of good versus bad carbohydrates. If your teen has trouble sleeping, encourage him to limit caffeine consumption to morning hours.

5. Chart your child's sleep. Many children with ADHD have trouble falling asleep, which can, in turn, worsen symptoms of inattention and focus. To get a handle on your child's sleep habits and what needs improving, keep a chart of when he goes to bed every night,

how much sleep he gets, how often he gets up at night, and when he wakes up in the morning. Make sure your child goes to bed at the same time every night and gets up at the same time every morning. He should avoid exercise, TV, computer/smartphone screens, and other stimulating activities for at least an hour before going to bed, and limit caffeine consumption to the morning hours. You may also want to avoid giving your child a heavy meal or snack right before bedtime. If your child still has sleep problems, talk to your physician about safe sleep medications or natural remedies for children.

6. Zone in on your child's stress triggers. If your child feels overwhelmed by feelings of stress, encourage him to list the biggest stresses in his day on a piece of paper, then help him start looking for ways to reduce or eliminate them. If your child can't eliminate the source of stress from his life, such as an overly demanding teacher or bully classmate, help your child change the way he reacts to it by role-playing challenging situations with him and rehearsing appropriate responses.

7. Find new ways to calm your child's body and soul. Do some simple meditation techniques with your child. Sit quietly, with your eyes closed, and focus on your breathing. Each time you exhale, silently repeat a one-syllable word—"one" or "peace" or "ohm." Experts suggest meditating for a few minutes or even for a few seconds every time you find yourself in a panic or funk. If your child can't sit still long enough to meditate, try a "moving" meditation, such as walking, tai chi, or yoga.

8. Help your child keep a lid on impulsive behavior. If your child has a tendency to say or do things he later regrets, such as interrupting or getting angry at others, encourage him to keep his impulses in check by counting to ten while breathing slowly, instead of acting out. Your child will be surprised to find that most of his impulses evaporate as quickly as they appeared.

9. Find constructive outlets for excess energy. Children with ADHD sometimes seem to have more nervous energy than other kids, and this hyperactivity needs to have an outlet of some sort. A hobby or other pastime can be helpful.

10. Keep up with the latest research on ADHD and strategies with online resources including professional journals, reputable newspapers such as the *New York Times*, and websites such as *www .chadd.org* or *www.addditudemag.com*.

Important Points to Consider

To be the best conscious parent possible, you have to take care of yourself as well as your child. Try doing these few things as often as possible:

1. Even when you feel like you don't have enough time, remind yourself that having a core mindfulness practice yourself will help you with parenting stress as well as allow your child to have a good role model for coping with stress.

2. Take at least ten minutes a day to dedicate toward your core practice. If you cannot seem to find ten minutes in your day, infuse a mindfulness mindset into the daily tasks you are already doing.

3. Set your phone's timer for a certain time of day for you to do your core practice, or use an app that will help remind you to do your core practice.

4. Don't let your practice slip. It is easy to get caught up in day-to-day survival mode, but even a few minutes a day can have a substantial impact on your psyche, energy, and enthusiasm for parenting.

CHAPTER 12

Choosing the Right Treatment

Although alleviating childhood ADHD symptoms is a top priority of treatment, the overall goal is to help your child function more efficiently, improve her quality of life, and help her cope with the demands of everyday life. Today, experts use many various therapies to treat childhood ADHD, including medication, psychotherapy, neurofeedback, drug-free alternatives, dietary intervention, exercise, relaxation techniques, and strategies to reinforce social skills. Because childhood ADHD is not one disorder but a cluster of syndromes, treatment plans are generally most effective when custom-tailored to meet the needs of individual children. Whatever treatment you choose for your child, incorporating conscious parenting techniques such as mindfulness and emotional awareness into your daily routine can help both you and your child live calmer, happier lives.

Evidence-Based Treatment Programs

Most ADHD experts agree that the best way to tackle ADHD is through a multitreatment approach that combines medication, psychotherapy, and social skills training.

Medication is generally regarded as the first line of defense in treating childhood ADHD, and is often so successful at alleviating symptoms that patients do little else to address them. Most ADHD experts agree, however, that "Pills do not substitute for skills."

Medication can certainly level the neurobiological playing field and allow children with ADHD to learn and develop the skills they need to succeed, but it won't always help them improve problems areas such as organization, time management, prioritizing, and using cognitive aids. For this reason, medication should be just one part of a child's treatment plan.

> You can have a direct impact on your child's social development by putting time aside to talk to her about behavior goals. ADHD medication can help manage your child's symptoms, but it doesn't take the place of one-on-one communication and support.

What to Try First

Most experts agree that ADHD medication is the best place to start when contemplating treatments for your child. Medications may offer the most immediate relief from symptoms and tend to have mild side effects that typically decrease over time. They are also more affordable—especially if your insurance company has a prescription drug program—and less time-consuming than treatments that require your child to interact with psychologists or psychiatrists on a regular basis.

Ask your doctor about the long-term effectiveness of the medication you are considering for your child. A study in 2014 in the *Journal of the American Academy of Child & Adolescent Psychiatry* showed that while most children with ADHD benefited from medication in the first year, for some children, the effects waned by the third year.

ADHD medications have also undergone years of stringent testing before being approved by the FDA, and are prescribed by licensed MDs or DOs. In some states, properly trained psychologists may also prescribe these medications. In addition, all FDA-approved medications have been subjected to a number of controlled scientific studies that measure their safety and effectiveness.

However, as a conscious parent, you should do your own homework and fully investigate any and all drugs you may be considering—not just reading the pharmaceutical companies' literature—before giving medications to your child. All drugs come with side effects and it is ultimately up to you to explore all options and ask questions of your child's doctor to get all the details.

With advances in medicine and methods for studying effectiveness, it may seem like new and contradictory information about medication for ADHD is being released every day. Remember that your job is not to be an expert, but rather to be an informed consumer. As a conscious parent, stay informed and continue to ask questions before deciding if medication is the first line of treatment for your child. If you are particularly wary of medication, the first step is to gather all the information you need to make an educated and thoughtful choice that is best for your child.

Some nondrug treatments for reducing ADHD symptoms have been studied, including dietary regimens, homeopathy, herbal medicine, Ayurveda and Chinese medicine, manipulation therapies, and sensory integration therapies. A few have been shown to be effective in controlled scientific studies, although more research is needed to understand the possible benefits of these treatments. Conscious parents may want to investigate research in these areas, especially if you are averse to putting your child on a drug-treatment regimen.

The research on mindfulness training is particularly promising as a nonpharmaceutical intervention. For example, a study published in 2013 in *Clinical Neurophysiology* conducted with adults found that mindfulness-based cognitive therapy (MBCT) had comparable neurophysiological effects related to attention and self-regulation as pharmacological treatments for ADHD.

There is certainly controversy and polarization surrounding traditional medicine and homeopathic and holistic treatment options for ADHD. Studies are often contradictory or inconclusive about so-called "alternative" treatments. However, it should be acknowledged that there is not as much funding for research concerning the effectiveness of holistic treatments, since pharmaceutical companies often provide funding for studies. The most important thing for conscious parents to know is that there are alternative treatments available, and it is your job to become educated about the safety and effectiveness. The same can be said for educating yourself about possible harmful side effects of traditional medicines. The bottom line is that becoming an informed consumer of treatment options, whether they are "traditional" or "alternative," is key.

Instead of thinking of medication options as either "traditional" or "alternative," weigh the evidence of effectiveness and safety of each choice. Have an open mind about your options and be sure to select a physician who is well versed in the research on both ends of the medication spectrum so you can make an informed choice.

Types of Psychological Treatments

Psychological treatments for childhood ADHD can help your child cope with the secondary symptoms of the disorder—in other words, the anger, frustration, hostility, impatience, low self-esteem, hopelessness, helplessness, guilt, blame, fear, and other feelings that rise from the primary symptoms of childhood ADHD, which include inattention, impulsivity, and hyperactivity. Behavior modification, a form of psychological therapy, may help your child with problem behaviors including failure to complete tasks such as getting dressed for school and controlling rage.

As a conscious parent, you want to give your child every chance possible to succeed. This often means trying different forms of treatment, and enlisting the help of a variety of professionals for advice. Don't hesitate to ask for help when you need it.

Some types of psychological treatment help your child see and understand why he is feeling the way he does. Others help him find ways to cope with the effects of living with the symptoms of ADHD, or modify his behavior and thoughts using conditioning and association. A number of different types of therapy may be used to support children with ADHD; some are discussed in Chapter 15.

- Talk Therapy. Counseling and psychotherapy can involve standard talk therapy, treatment that teaches your child how to change the way he thinks and acts, and therapies that enable him to act out or vent pent-up feelings.

- Cognitive-Behavior Therapy (CBT). Typically used with older children and teens, CBT operates on the premise "change your thoughts, change your feelings and behavior." Your child learns to identify patterns of thought and behavior. She also learns techniques to modify them, such as replacing self-destructive thoughts with more realistic and constructive thoughts.

○ Awareness Training. Your child works with a counselor to develop increased awareness of himself and his environment. The goal of awareness training is to help your child become more in tune with how he thinks, feels, and acts. Unlike cognitive-behavior therapy, in which your child examines thoughts and feelings before he acts, awareness training teaches him to pay attention to his thoughts, feelings, and behavior at every moment. Tapping into this "streaming" information can help him consciously change the way he behaves.

○ Psycho-Educational Counseling. This type of counseling is like taking a course in ADHD, with an emphasis on teaching you and your child about the many aspects of ADHD so you can both better understand the disorder, and find new skills for living with it. In psycho-educational counseling, your child's counselor acts more as a teacher who enlightens you and your child about ADHD, rather than as a therapist.

○ Group Therapy. In group therapy, a group of people with similar problems meets with a therapist to discuss problems, share experiences, and find solutions. They usually meet for a specific amount of time so group members can become more comfortable with each other, and establish bonds.

○ Family Therapy. In family counseling, the entire family meets with a therapist to better understand family members with ADHD, to find family solutions for creating harmony at home, and to learn ways to support family members with the disorder.

Will counseling help alleviate your child's ADHD symptoms? Counseling and psychotherapy can't eliminate the symptoms of childhood ADHD, but they can help your child develop strategies to better cope with symptoms. Counseling can help your child accept the fact that he has ADHD and help him adjust his personal and school life so things go more smoothly.

BEHAVIOR THERAPY FOR BEHAVIOR IMPROVEMENT

Behavior modification is another effective treatment, though like neurofeedback, it requires ongoing work with a therapist. Most therapists work with not only the child, but also the parents and family members, so you will likely gain knowledge that can be applied immediately to help your child with ADHD as well as the other children in the household. Some behavioral therapies are based on research on learning in animals, in which there is less emphasis on thoughts and more emphasis on techniques for rewarding changes in behavior. Cognitive-behavior therapy integrates changing your child's thoughts to change her behavior, but may also incorporate rewards, as in behavioral therapy. For more information on behavior modification, see Chapter 14.

DEVELOPING SPECIFIC SKILLS THROUGH TRAINING

Training is a form of counseling that helps kids with ADHD develop or improve specific skills they may need in a variety of situations, including school, college, and work. It is also a valuable type of therapy for children and teens who aren't comfortable with approaches used in standard talk therapy.

During training, instead of examining your child's emotions and what motivates him to think and behave in a certain way, he will focus exclusively on improving or developing concrete skills needed to function in a more efficient way.

Training is a type of counseling that focuses on parts of your child's life where he needs to develop specific skills, abilities, and talents. Counselors as well as ADHD coaches use training to help your child develop the organizational, academic, and planning skills he needs to succeed at school, college, and at work.

Although training doesn't alleviate ADHD symptoms, many participants discover that developing new skills helps them think and act in a more positive and life-affirming way. As a result, they find themselves functioning more efficiently and appropriately at school or college and in social settings.

Neurofeedback Therapies

Many ADHD experts believe neurofeedback is one of the most effective ways to treat childhood ADHD today. A review paper on EEG biofeedback for ADHD published in 2005 identified multiple published group studies in which the benefits of neurofeedback were either comparable to or exceeded benefits seen in patients treated with stimulant medication. Children with ADHD experience lower activity in specific areas of their brains than their peers without the disorder. Neurofeedback, also known as EEG biofeedback, is an exercise program for the brain that aims to help your child change his brainwave patterns at will. As your child repeatedly achieves a more "normal" balance of different types of brain activity, his brain establishes conditions that reinforce new activities, which makes it more likely that he will function in a different way.

During neurofeedback, your child is hooked up to an EEG machine, and electrodes attached to his scalp (painlessly) deliver a baseline report of his brain activity. Your child's baseline report is then compared against a databank of "normal" baselines to measure differences.

Your child will repeatedly perform learning exercises (usually computer games) aimed at improving areas where his brain function is weak; the computer programs respond to changes he makes to his brain patterns. Children receive real-time feedback on their brainwave activity and learn how to alter their typical EEG patterns to one that is consistent with a more focused and attentive state. As your child improves his score, he repeatedly alters his brainwaves to achieve a desired balance, teaching his brain how to create conditions that compensate for ADHD.

Short-term benefits cited by proponents of neurofeedback include improved attention, focus, and concentration. Your child may also gain more ability to complete tasks, an increase in organizational skills, and a reduction in impulsivity and hyperactivity.

Neurofeedback is more expensive than typical drug therapy and requires that your child work with a therapist on a weekly basis for several weeks, though this treatment may provide good results. Neurofeedback may be a good choice for your child if you are hesitant to use medication.

It's important to exercise care when choosing a neurofeedback therapist for your child. The practitioner should ideally be licensed in psychology or in a field related to medicine, and her license should allow for independent practice. She should ideally be a state-licensed, PhD-level psychologist with training in brain anatomy and function, and be certified by the Behavior Certification International Alliance.

Balancing and Holistic Therapies

Many children and teens with ADHD also use balancing and holistic therapies such as chiropractic, osteopathy, yoga, meditation, acupuncture, acupressure, and homeopathy to reduce stress, to slow racing thoughts, and to experience feelings of calm and tranquility.

Treatments include sensory integration therapies, which allege to help your child process stimuli more effectively. Auditory integration training is designed to assist with the processing of auditory stimuli. In this therapy, the child listens to specially filtered and modulated music, designed to address hypersensitivities that are believed to interfere with the child's attention. Vision therapy is geared to help improve visual processing by training the child using in-office and at-home eye exercises.

Although the results of these therapies have not been scientifically documented, some children and teens with ADHD find them extremely helpful in alleviating symptoms. These therapies are not usually prescribed in lieu of other biological treatments, but they may be useful complements to your child's ADHD treatment program.

Proponents of such treatments say that they may be worth pursuing in the event conventional treatments fail, if only because they seem to have worked for so many others throughout the years, or, in some cases, throughout the ages. Practices such as yoga, tai chi, mindfulness, and meditation may help relieve restlessness, hyperactivity, and depression caused by childhood ADHD. Studies and personal testimonies show that slowing breathing and staying in the "now" via meditation, yoga, and mindfulness have helped people feel calmer, clearer, saner, more empowered, more confident, and far more centered.

The link between meditation and improved brain functioning in children with ADHD was documented in *Mind & Brain, the Journal of Psychiatry* in 2011. The researchers found that middle school students diagnosed with ADHD who meditated twice a day in school had reduced symptoms of ADHD, stress, and anxiety, as well as increased language-processing skills.

Studies done at medical facilities and university research centers are beginning to provide strong scientific data about the benefits of meditation, yoga, and other mindfulness practices on ADHD. Over 500 studies on mindfulness/meditation and the brain are now included in the National Institute of Mental Health's (NIMH) PubMed database. The NIMH is the largest scientific organization in the world, and it presents many studies that investigate mindfulness as a complementary treatment for a range of mental health conditions. This indicates that mindfulness is rapidly moving from an "experimental" treatment to a bona fide research-based treatment.

A study published in 2012 in *Frontiers in Human Neuroscience* showed that mindfulness seems to flex the brain circuitry for sustaining attention. The researchers imaged the brains of meditators while they went through four basic mental movements: focusing on a chosen target, noticing that their minds had wandered, bringing their minds back to the target, and sustaining their focus there. Meditation helped adult patients strengthen the neural circuitry for keeping attention and focus.

The bottom line about so-called alternative treatments is that you want to be careful about where you place your hope and your money when it comes to treatment for your child. Most people do not have the background or the information to know whether medical and psychological treatments are likely to be effective.

The best approach is to start with therapy that well-conducted scientific research has already shown to be likely to benefit childhood ADHD. In psychology and medicine, there is a sense that every therapy seems to work for someone. Every approach has its very opinionated proponents.

However, claims by practitioners and even patients' dramatic personal stories are not sufficient evidence for efficacy. This is a very important point. There are always practitioners and patients who claim that their experiences with a certain approach proves that it is effective. They are usually sincere, but sincerity is often not enough. It is best to take a guarded approach to any therapy and consult with your physician before incorporating something into your child's treatment program.

Diet and Exercise

Eating a diet low in simple carbohydrates, such as sugar and starch, and high in dietary protein, as well as engaging in regular aerobic exercise, are two nonmedical ways that may keep childhood ADHD symptoms at bay, although there is no scientific evidence that eating certain foods alleviates or cures childhood ADHD.

EXERCISE AS MEDICINE?

If your child or teen has ADHD and is also a couch potato, your physician may suggest that she embark on a regular program of aerobic exercise such as walking, hiking, swimming, team sports, or cycling.

Aerobic exercise will firm up flab and tone your child's muscles, but it's equally healthy for your child's brain. Just a half-hour of exercise four times a week increases your child's brain levels of dopamine, norepinephrine, and serotonin—three neurotransmitters that not only improve focus and attention, but enhance feelings of well-being.

Research shows that extremely active teens with ADHD, such as marathon runners or triathletes, may not need to take stimulant drugs to enjoy symptom relief. Studies show that regular intense exercise decreases ADHD symptoms by causing the brain to release the same neurotransmitters that are activated by stimulant drugs.

Exercise is also the ultimate empowerment tool, reducing feelings of helpless and hopelessness and making your child feel like she can conquer, if not the world, then at least her ADHD symptoms.

FEEL-GOOD ENDORPHINS

Because exercise also releases serotonin, the "feel-good" hormone, your child is also likely to feel less stressed, more centered, and more at peace with the world when she exercises regularly. Your child or teen can time her workout for the benefit she's seeking. She should exercise in the morning to jump-start her day and get herself moving, and work out in late afternoon to unwind and improve the quality of her sleep (but not within an hour of bedtime).

IMPORTANCE OF "GREEN TIME"

Research, including several studies reported by *Healthline* in 2012, shows that children with ADHD enjoy a reduction in symptoms when they spend time playing outdoors in nature. If you live in a city, take your child to a park with grass and trees. If you live in the suburbs or the country, encourage your child to play in yards with trees, flowers, and grass, rather than in concrete playgrounds or streets. Or take your child hiking through forests.

IMPORTANCE OF GETTING ENOUGH SLEEP

Because of their hyperactivity, many children with ADHD need more sleep than other children. Unfortunately, attention deficits can cause overstimulation and make it difficult for them to fall asleep. Here are a few strategies to help your child get the sleep she needs:

- Make sure your child goes to bed at the same time every night.

- Increase your child's physical activity level, and decrease the time she spends in front of the television or computer.

- Reduce the caffeine level of your child's diet by limiting cola drinks, sports drinks with caffeine, tea, and chocolate.

- Help your child wind down by creating a buffer zone an hour before bedtime when she does quiet activities, such as reading or coloring.

- Use white noise or relaxation recordings to help your child unwind and fall asleep.

- Help your child do a mindfulness activity before bedtime, such as a guided imagery recording, deep breathing, or meditation.

Benefits of a Multitreatment Approach

Most ADHD experts agree that the best approach for treating childhood ADHD is using a combination of medication, psychotherapy, and behavior modification.

Using a variety of different treatments increases the chances your child will enjoy more continuous relief from symptoms in the event one or more of her treatments are no longer effective, stop working on a temporary basis, or she needs to stop one or more treatments for whatever reason. Using a combination of treatments makes sure your child always has some treatment to fall back on.

Tools for Charting Your Child's Progress

Staying on top of symptoms, medications, and treatments as well as the many other details of your child's life requires a great deal of organization, planning, and attention to detail—some of the very things your child or teen may have trouble with. Here are some easy ways to help you and your child with ADHD stay on top of things:

○ Invest in a day calendar that has a large enough space for each day so you and/or your child can keep track of various and sundry details. Break it up into home, work, and personal, and put notes, tips, and reminders under each category—from doctor's appointments and important phone numbers, to reactions to medications, stress-busting strategies, and school assignment deadlines.

○ Have your child keep a diary. Keeping a diary or day journal is a great way for your child or teen with ADHD to relieve stress, rant and rave, and record private thoughts and emotions she may not be comfortable discussing with you or others. Once she writes something down, it's not only off her chest, but it also helps her look at thoughts or actions more objectively. Because remembering things may not be your child's forte, a journal can also help her stay on top of important dates and occasions. You'll also find a variety of apps available to record thoughts and feelings experienced throughout the day, such as Gratitude Journal and iDiary.

○ Create a medications journal to record when, why, and how your child's symptoms wax and wane, her reactions to new medications, variations in mood based on slight variations in dosages, how various treatments make your child feel, and which treatments work and don't work for her. Beware that missing a dose or taking two doses at once to catch up on missed doses can have negative consequences. Before seeing your doctor, make a list of questions you or your child want to ask him along with a list of medications your child is taking. If your child is exhibiting side effects or other problems related to medication, speak to your health-care provider as soon as possible.

○ Have your child create a daily "mood" chart with categories for exercise, hours of sunshine, sleep, nutrition, and stress relief. Have her rate her mood on a scale of one to ten, then engage in activities designed to increase relaxation and happiness. She can give herself a check for thirty minutes of daily exercise, thirty minutes of sunshine, seven hours of sleep, a healthy diet low in sugar and carbohydrates, and engaging in stress-reducing activities. There are also a variety of apps available for older children for tracking mood and self-care activities, such as iMoodJournal and DBSA Wellness Tracker.

O Have your child become a list-master. Have her create lists of daily tasks she needs to achieve, and then have her strike them off as she completes them to achieve a sense of accomplishment. If your adolescent or teen has problems keeping her class schedule straight, have her list the classes in chronological order, along with a note as to when each class begins and ends. This will help your child correct scheduling conflicts before they occur.

Important Points to Consider

Along with traditional treatments for ADHD, incorporating awareness practices into your child's daily routine will help her feel more in control of her symptoms.

1. Encourage your child to write down how she feels on a daily basis so she can see exactly how her moods change from day to day.

2. Keep a list and calendar of medications. Spend time going over the calendar and lists with your child so she feels included in her treatment plan.

3. Sleep is essential for children with ADHD. Using relaxation recordings or a white noise sound maker can help your child wind down after a particularly stressful day.

4. In addition to cardio-based exercises that will help your child break a sweat, suggest that she try yoga and tai chi. Maybe even offer to try these exercises with her.

 **CHAPTER 13**

Treating with Medication

Medications for childhood ADHD basically work by impacting the neurotransmitters in your child's brain that are responsible for attention and motivation. Stimulant drugs have long been considered the first line of defense in treating the disorder and are still widely regarded as the most effective, however, many nonstimulant drugs, including antidepressants, anticonvulsants, waking agents, and even estrogen, have proven beneficial in treating childhood ADHD symptoms. Many experts believe that Strattera, a nonstimulant drug recently approved for treating ADHD, will eventually replace stimulant drugs and become the standard treatment for the disorder. When your child begins taking medication for her ADHD, it is important that you monitor her progress. Focus on her behavior and mood, and talk to her about how she is feeling. Nurturing your child emotionally during this transition is essential.

Results of NIH Landmark Study on Results of Medication and Therapy

The National Institute of Mental Health's Multimodal Treatment of ADHD (MTA) study was the first major multi-site trial comparing different treatments for ADHD. The study, originally published in 1999, involved nearly 600 children, age seven to nine, and the same cohort of children are followed up on over time to provide information about long-term trends. The initial findings indicated that most children with ADHD had significant benefits from stimulant medications, including a reduction in core ADHD symptoms of hyperactivity, inattention, and impulsivity. Data also showed that children taking stimulant medications enjoyed an improvement in academic performance, a decrease in disruptive and aggressive behavior, and an improvement in their relationships with friends, peers, and family members, according to David Rabiner, PhD, research professor with Duke University.

In 2007, a follow-up study was conducted with the same subjects who were then teenagers. The researchers found the high school youths' functioning remained improved overall compared to their functioning at the beginning of the study, though compared to peers without ADHD, they still showed significantly more social and academic problems. Interestingly, many of the youths who had taken medication in the early phases of the study had stopped taking medication, which may suggest that using medication may lose either appeal or effectiveness over time. More research is needed, but the researcher pointed to a need for further exploration of alternative treatments. They indicated that medication might continue to be helpful for some teenagers, but that their needs should be revisited and periodically re-evaluated.

COMBINED TREATMENT BENEFITS

Children in the combined treatment group received both medication and behavior modification. By the end of the study, children in the combined group could take less medication than those receiving just medication.

Although children taking medication had fewer ADHD symptoms than children who only received behavior modification, medication did not reduce symptoms of oppositional behavior, enhance relationships with other children, or improve academic performance.

MORE RESEARCH NEEDED

Experts agree that more research is needed to study the long-term effectiveness of stimulant medication in children. New nonstimulant medications are, in many cases, proving to be as effective as stimulant medication, although like any medication, they also have side effects. The benefits and side effects of stimulant and nonstimulant medications will be discussed later in this chapter.

Pros and Cons of Medication in Young Children

Stimulant medication is not a universal panacea for childhood ADHD. Although most children will see improvements, academic challenges and behavior problems may persist that require other types of intervention. And studies show that stimulant medications do not work for all children with ADHD.

> Deciding whether to put your child on medication for his ADHD is a difficult task. Before you become too overwhelmed, refocus your attention on the benefits your child may see from taking medication. It is very easy to get caught up in the negative and forget the positive.

Although most children do not suffer longtime adverse side effects from taking stimulant medication when taken properly, it's important for parents and children to monitor side effects and bring unexpected or adverse side effects to the attention of your physician.

MYTHS ABOUT ADHD MEDICATION

There are many myths concerning stimulant medications. Before letting the myths discourage or frighten you from considering the use of stimulant medications for your child, it's important to get to the truth of the matter.

Here are two of the most popular myths concerning ADHD medication for children, and the truth behind the issues:

O Myth 1: Children treated with stimulant medication are likely to become addicted to it and also more likely to abuse other drugs. Truth: There is no data indicating that children with ADHD who take stimulant medications are more likely to abuse drugs than other children. In fact, studies show just the opposite—that they are less inclined to abuse drugs.

O Myth 2: Stimulant medications will turn your child into a zombie. Truth: Some children may become sluggish and withdrawn when going on medication, but these symptoms are generally an indication that the dose is too high, or that the child is suffering from a coexisting condition that has not been addressed. In fact, studies show that children treated with stimulant medication show an increase in social behavior, not a decrease.

Parents are sometimes uncomfortable with using medication with their children as the first course of action, despite research findings about its effectiveness. This is a common hesitation. The best way to decide whether or not you want to use medication is to get as much information as possible about medications and other treatments, and weigh the information as objectively as possible. Acknowledge to yourself that this is a difficult decision and seek consultation and support throughout the process to ease the stress of weighing the pros and cons of medication.

THE PRACTICE OF POLYPHARMACY

Polypharmacy, or prescribing several psychiatric medications at the same time, is often used to treat coexisting conditions in children with ADHD. For instance, if a child has ADHD as well as clinical anxiety, depression, or bipolar disorder, he may need to take medication for both conditions. If done in the right way, polypharmacy can result in a simultaneous reduction of symptoms for both conditions.

But if medications are prescribed without taking into account their side effects, a patient could suffer serious medical consequences, or even experience an increase in ADHD symptoms if one or both medications have side effects such as depression, anxiety, brain fog, or insomnia.

Most Commonly Prescribed Drugs for Childhood ADHD

Over the past fifteen years or so, the medication options for treating childhood ADHD have greatly expanded. Today, the most popular medications for treating the disease include many different stimulant drugs, and a wide variety of nonstimulant drugs in various drug categories.

THE POPULARITY OF STIMULANTS

Despite the growing number of medication options, stimulant medications, including methylphenidate (such as Ritalin), and dextroamphetamine compounds (such as Dextrostat, Dexedrine Spansule, and Adderall) remain the most commonly prescribed drugs for childhood ADHD. Many experts also believe they are the most effective.

ANTIDEPRESSANTS

Although stimulant medications such as Ritalin and Adderall remain the most frequently prescribed drugs, they are no longer the only line of defense for children with ADHD. Other medications that are sometimes prescribed off-label for ADHD include tricyclic antidepressants (TCAs), such as Elavil. Medications that may be prescribed for comorbid conditions include selective serotonin reuptake inhibitors, such as Prozac, Zoloft, and others. Although no antidepressants have been approved by the FDA for treating childhood ADHD, they may be prescribed "off-label" to alleviate its symptoms. Again, they should be used with caution in children and adolescents.

NONSTIMULANT DRUGS

In 2002, the nonstimulant drug Strattera became the first medication approved by the FDA specifically for the treatment of ADHD in adults, and is also used to treat childhood ADHD. Because Strattera is not a Class II stimulant, experts believe that there is also no abuse potential.

The Right Drug at the Right Dose

Drug treatment for childhood ADHD requires that you maintain an open line of communication with your medical experts to ensure your child is taking the right drug at the right dose, and to take corrective measures in the event your child suffers adverse side effects or a drug stops working for her.

It's important to keep in mind that medications are not magic bullets or cures, but part of an overall treatment approach. Because the first medication your child takes may not be the drug that offers her the most benefits, it's important to pay attention to how medications affect your child's symptoms, and what side effects occur.

Remember that you and your doctor may need to experiment with various medications before you find the medication, amount, and dosing schedule that works best for your child, so be patient.

DOSAGE CONCERNS

Research funded by the National Institute of Mental Health also indicates that medication is most effective when treatment is routinely monitored by your physician. Children may also benefit from a change in dose or scheduling. Long-acting medications that are taken once a day, rather than in multiple doses, seem to work best for most children.

If your child's ADHD symptoms are relatively mild, she may only need to take medication during the school year. If she has a severe form of ADHD, she may need to stay on medication year-round. Consult with your physician to determine the best course of action for your child.

HOW LONG SHOULD YOUR CHILD TAKE MEDICATION?

Physicians advise that most children take medication only as long as it is deemed helpful and necessary. Some children "grow out of" ADHD to the point that they no longer need medication. Others suffer from ADHD symptoms as adolescents and adults. Your physician will probably re-evaluate your child's ADHD and medication plan every year to determine if she still needs to take medication, or if the dose needs to be adjusted as your child grows.

According to recent controlled studies, people who took higher doses of stimulant drugs had better results in 70 percent of cases than those who took lower amounts of the same drugs. As blood levels of the stimulant fell, symptoms of ADHD rebounded, and resulted in more intense symptoms as well as increased irritability, according to the studies.

SHORT- VERSUS LONG-DURATION DRUGS

Short-duration stimulants may wear off quickly. Given that many children have problems with forgetfulness, taking multiple doses during the day can leave them unprotected if they forget to take the second and third doses.

Taking ADHD stimulants at night to help children calm down may leave them feeling so relaxed they can't focus on homework. If you notice your child having a hard time, it is time to talk to her doctor about a dose change.

In general, medications with gradual onset of effect and long durations of effect in the body before they are excreted are likely to work most smoothly, without causing emotional ups and downs. These are also the best formulations for children and teens with a history of substance abuse as they avoid the "hit" and "buzz" of recreational stimulants.

Stimulant Medications

The most frequently prescribed, and also among the most effective drugs, stimulants come in a variety of forms and brands. Under medical supervision, stimulant medications are considered safe, and when used as prescribed, they do not make children with ADHD feel "high."

Although the majority of children with ADHD, 60–80 percent, enjoy a dramatic decrease in symptoms, some only get some benefits, and others reap none at all. Others suffer from side effects that are so severe that they must go off the drugs.

Fears that stimulants lead to drug abuse or addiction have largely been silenced by controlled studies.

HOW STIMULANTS WORK IN THE BRAIN

Stimulant medications are believed to directly affect the brain neurotransmitters dopamine and norepinephrine, which are responsible for transmitting messages between different parts of the brain.

Dopamine controls the volume or power of the signals coming into your brain as well as areas of the brain that control filtering and screening—or what you pay attention to. Norepinephrine controls your level of alertness, clarity, and wakefulness. Both neurotransmitters have an impact on motivation.

These neurotransmitters are also believed to affect attention and behavior symptoms, although how each neurotransmitter contributes to the alleviation of symptoms remains unknown.

Generic stimulants are usually inexpensive, although many long-acting stimulants can be quite expensive if your insurance doesn't cover medication costs.

Although about three-quarters of children with ADHD also have coexisting conditions, there is a lack of controlled studies on the most effective ways to treat children with coexisting or overlapping conditions. To arrive at the best approach, physicians must rely on their previous therapeutic and clinical experience, and continual feedback from patients.

FORMS OF STIMULANT MEDICATION

Stimulant medications come in different forms, such as a pill, capsule, liquid, or skin patch. Some medications also come in short-acting, long-acting, or extended-release varieties. In each of these varieties, the active ingredient is the same, but it is released differently in the body.

Long-acting or extended-release forms ("ER" or "XR") often work best for children who need continuous relief during daytime and evening hours, and who may be too forgetful or distracted to remember to take second and third doses. They are also prescribed to children and teens who have abused other drugs or who are at high risk for substance abuse.

THE HALF-LIFE OF MEDICATION

The half-life of a drug is the time it takes for one-half of the quantity of the drug to be eliminated from the body. It is a measure of the duration of its activity in the body. Neglecting to take drugs on time that have a short half-life may result in a condition called discontinuation syndrome. Symptoms include irritability, insomnia, dizziness, light-headedness, and flu-like symptoms, and may persist for weeks.

COMMONLY PRESCRIBED STIMULANTS

There are many different kinds of stimulant drugs your physician may prescribe for your child. Although they all work in a similar fashion, they differ in how quickly they begin to work, how long they remain in your child's bloodstream, the degree of relief they provide, and their side effects. Through trial and error, you and your physician will be able to determine which medication(s) work best for your child.

O Methylphenidate. Marketed as Ritalin, Concerta, Metadate, and Focalin, methylphenidate is one of the most widely prescribed drugs for ADHD and is available in a wide range of forms. Different brands use different delivery systems to get the medication into your child's system. There are also differences among brands in how long the drugs take to reach their half-life and peak, and how long they remain in the bloodstream.

O Dexedrine (d-amphetamine). One of the oldest drugs used to treat ADHD and still considered one of the best, Dexedrine is marketed in both short-acting and sustained-released forms.

O Adderall (salts of d- and l-amphetamine). Similar to Dexedrine, this medication is believed to have more impact on norepinephrine than Dexedrine. It is marketed in short- and long-acting forms.

O Vyvanse. A newer medication, it is similar to Adderall in its chemical composition. It is believed to have less potential for substance abuse than most stimulants because snorting it or injecting it will not cause a user to get high. Before it can become effective, it must undergo a conversion in the body from its oral form to a stimulant form. It may result in a smoother onset and less restlessness than Adderall.

O Desoxyn (methamphetamine). Biologically identical to the illegal "meth" made in drug labs, Desoxyn has gotten an undeserved bad reputation. The legal, prescription form of Desoxyn is not only one of the most beneficial medications for many children with ADHD, but also one of the least expensive medications.

SIDE EFFECTS OF STIMULANTS

The most common adverse reactions to stimulants in clinical trials in adult patients were decreased appetite, headache, dry mouth, nausea, insomnia, anxiety, dizziness, weight loss, and irritability. The most common adverse reactions associated with discontinuation from adult clinical trials were anxiety, irritability, insomnia, and blood pressure increases. However, it should be noted that most side effects are minor and disappear over time, or if the dosage level is lowered.

DEALING WITH STIMULANT-RELATED SLEEP PROBLEMS

If your child can't fall asleep, ask your doctor about prescribing a lower dose of the medication or a shorter-acting form for use in the afternoon or early evening. You might also ask about having your child take the medication earlier in the day, or stopping the afternoon or evening dose.

Maintaining good sleep hygiene is also important, and includes going to bed and rising at the same time every day, ending the day with relaxing activities, and establishing a relaxing sleep environment. Using black-out eye shades, ear plugs, and white-noise machines can help eliminate sleep-robbing distractions such as bright lights and noise.

Incorporating a deep breathing practice into your child's bedtime routine can help you and your child relax at the end of a long day. Simply breathing in for four seconds, and then breathing out for four seconds can have a calming effect.

Nonstimulant Medications

Although nonstimulants such as antidepressants and mood stabilizers have been used for years to alleviate symptoms of ADHD, few have created the excitement and buzz as nonstimulant medications. Strattera is the first nonstimulant medication approved by the FDA for ADHD, and also the first medication approved by the FDA for adults, as well as children.

Strattera works like an antidepressant to strengthen the chemical signal between nerves that use the neurotransmitter norepinephrine to send messages. Unlike selective serotonin reuptake inhibitors (SSRIs), Strattera does not have an impact on serotonin levels in the brain.

Despite its high price, Strattera may be helpful to children who cannot tolerate stimulants, although some patients claim the effects are not as strong as those provided by stimulant drugs. However, there have been indications that Strattera may rarely increase suicidal thinking and that it might also trigger mania. It should be used with care in children, and as with all medications, under the guidance of a qualified physician.

The medication is taken once a day, although those suffering gastrointestinal upset can take a smaller dose twice a day. Full effects are usually felt within four to six weeks, and last all day or even into the next morning. In long-term studies, two-thirds of people taking Strattera enjoyed relief from symptoms for longer than thirty-four weeks.

Common side effects include headache, abdominal pain, nausea, vomiting, weight loss, anxiety, sleepiness, and insomnia. Strattera can also interfere with sexual performance in adults.

Antidepressants

With the exception of Strattera, most other nonstimulant medications are generally considered second-line medications for ADHD. They tend to be used in children who had a poor or bad response to stimulants, couldn't tolerate the side effects, or who have coexisting psychiatric conditions that rule out taking stimulant drugs.

A WARNING ABOUT ANTIDEPRESSANTS

Though the picture is not clear, keep in mind when considering the use of antidepressant medications that suicidal thinking has been found to be a relatively rare side effect in children and adolescents in at least some studies. This does not mean that these medications should not be used at all, though in reality they are rarely used for treating ADHD in children and adolescents. A risk-versus-benefit approach based on your child's specific needs and treatment history is highly recommended. Work with your physician to monitor any negative side effects, including any aberrations in thinking and behavior.

SELECTIVE SEROTONIN REUPTAKE INHIBITORS (SSRIS)

Prescribed for depression, anxiety, and obsessive-compulsive disorder as well as for controlling anger and aggression, SSRIs are most useful in alleviating coexisting symptoms of conditions accompanying ADHD. They work primarily by eliminating serotonin from the brain's synapses, though they may affect other neurotransmitters to a lesser degree as well.

Popular SSRIs include Prozac, the oldest SSRI, with a long half-life but many known drug interactions; Luvox, which is similar to Prozac but has a shorter half-life and fewer drug reactions; Paxil, a short-acting SSRI that may pose problems with dosing and discontinuation syndrome; and Zoloft, another short-acting SSRI that may also offer some of the benefits of stimulant drugs, but can cause discontinuation syndrome problems.

SSRIs have a variety of side effects, many of which are mild or which affect a small percentage of people. The most troublesome side effects may include weight gain, drowsiness, irritability, and thinning hair or hair loss.

Other SSRIs sometimes prescribed to children with ADHD include Celexa and Lexapro. Both have longer half-lives than other SSRIs except Prozac, and fewer drug reactions than most SSRIs as well. Lexapro, which is similar to Celexa, is often preferred by patients and physicians because it is more potent and has fewer side effects.

SEROTONIN/NOREPINEPHRINE REUPTAKE INHIBITORS

These antidepressants have an impact on the levels of both serotonin and norepinephrine, and are useful in treating depression, anxiety, and ADHD. However, they generally don't offer the symptom relief of stimulant drugs, and are often prescribed when stimulant drugs don't work, or in addition to stimulant drugs.

One widely prescribed drug in this category is Effexor, which seems to stimulate energy as well as lead to a calming feeling.

Although there are no controlled studies on the use of Effexor in children with ADHD, several noncontrolled studies indicate that it may be especially helpful in treating ADHD with coexisting depression and/or anxiety. However, side effects of higher doses may increase blood pressure, and sudden discontinuation of Effexor could lead to nausea and vomiting.

Another popular drug in this category is Remeron, which works on serotonin, norepinephrine, and histamine to promote sleep, increase energy, and increase appetite. However, one major side effect is a dramatic increase in appetite, and a constant craving for carbohydrates. Everything else being equal, Remeron can be a great medication for your child if he is small or has a poor appetite. But if your child is already overweight, Remeron could make it even harder for him to shed unwanted pounds, and, in fact, could lead to him gain weight.

TRICYCLIC ANTIDEPRESSANTS (TCAS)

Tricyclic antidepressants (TCAs), the first medications developed to treat depression, work by inhibiting serotonin and norepinephrine reuptake significantly.

TCAs have negligible risk of abuse, and are especially beneficial when treating children with ADHD who also have coexisting anxiety and depression. On the down side, it may take several weeks for these drugs to have a full clinical effect, and TCAs generally don't offer the relief of stimulants.

TCAs prescribed for ADHD include Elavil, Sinequan, and nortriptyline, all of which have sedating qualities (Elavil has the strongest sedation qualities, nortriptyline has the least).

Another TCA, Norpramin, has proven beneficial in children with ADHD when given in small doses. Anafranil, another TCA, has an impact on serotonin levels and is often prescribed for children with ADHD who also suffer from compulsive disorders.

Side effects of TCAs range from sleepiness and constipation to light-headedness and dry mouth, although more serious conditions include cardiac problems, and possible death by overdose.

Mood Stabilizers and Antihypertensives

Mood stabilizers, traditionally used to treat bipolar disorder or to reduce or prevent seizure, are also prescribed by psychiatrists to help modulate irritability and rapid mood shifts. The most widely prescribed mood stabilizers include lithium, Depakote, Tegretol, and Lamictal.

ANTIHYPERTENSIVES

Antihypertensives are used to decrease hyperactivity and impulsivity in children with ADHD, and may also help relieve insomnia. Drugs commonly prescribed for ADHD symptoms include Catapres, guanfacine, and various beta-blockers, including atenolol.

INTUNIV/GUANFACINE/TENEX

A new nonstimulant drug prescribed for childhood ADHD, Intuniv is the extended-release form of guanfacine, which is also sold under the brand name Tenex. Intuniv has recently been approved for use in children and adolescents with ADHD.

Intuniv shows a lot of promise in controlling symptoms often associated with ADHD, particularly rage, argumentativeness, and irritability, as well as the more common symptoms of ADHD. It can also be safely used with other medications, including stimulant medications.

Some anecdotal reports have been very encouraging. Intuniv provides an alternative or adjunct to stimulant treatment, but is probably not a first-line treatment in most cases.

Tenex and Catapres are also sometimes prescribed to eliminate tics, impulsivity, or aggression. Because of its sedating properties, Catapres is frequently prescribed for children with ADHD and insomnia.

Both mood stabilizers and antihypertensives require closer medical monitoring. Blood tests, and sometimes an EKG, may also be required.

Other Medications for Childhood ADHD

In addition to the previous categories of medications, a few others have been used with varying degrees of success to treat symptoms of ADHD.

- Desyrel (trazodone). The atypical antidepressant Desyrel (trazodone) is a mild antidepressant that may be prescribed to children with ADHD who have trouble falling asleep.

- BuSpar. A serotonin stabilizer usually prescribed to control anxiety and anger, BuSpar is prescribed to control anxiety in children with ADHD.

- Nicotinic analogues. These medications act on some of the same brain receptors as nicotine, and may also provide some relief. Although most research on ADHD has revolved around regulating the balance of neurotransmitters, some researchers believe poor regulation of the nicotinic receptors may also be involved.

Short- and Long-Term Benefits

Whether your child has just been diagnosed with ADHD, or is taking a medication for the first time, sometimes it can be hard to figure out what constitutes a positive reaction to a drug. You may wonder if it's the medication or something else that is making your child feel better, or which negative side effects are worth mentioning to your physician.

Research shows that taking the right medications in the right dosage can make all the difference in the world when it comes to normalizing behavior in children with ADHD. According to a study conducted by the National Institute of Mental Health, those under a physician's care taking proper medication enjoy normal function 85 percent of the time.

Your child's reaction to medication may be immediate or happen over time, depending on the type of medication and its dosage. In fact, there are many signs that a medication is working. These include:

- Being better able to pay attention

- Feeling less distracted

- Being better able to recall things

- Getting things done on time more often

- Feeling less restless and jittery

- Tending to think before acting instead of blurting things out

- Having more control over emotions and moods

- Suffering fewer and less severe mood swings

- Displaying less erratic behavior

- Having more motivation

- Having an easier time starting things and getting things done

- Getting a better night's sleep

- Finding it easier to make and keep friends

- Feeling less tempted to engage in reckless behavior, such as drinking or taking drugs

Managing Side Effects

Although almost every medication has side effects, not everyone has the same reaction to the same medication. Some people may barely notice side effects whereas others may be so bothered by them that they have to stop taking the drug or take a lower dosage.

Regardless of how mild or severe your child's ADHD symptoms, or whether or not your child also has coexisting or overlapping conditions, it's important to find medication(s) that not only alleviate her symptoms, but facilitate her physical, emotional, and mental health.

WHEN TO CALL YOUR DOCTOR

In some cases, side effects are the body's warning signal that your child and the drug are not compatible. In others, side effects only manifest temporarily. In either case, you'll want to keep your physician abreast of them. If your child suffers from one or more of the following side effects, contact your doctor:

- Personality changes. If your child is normally sunny and upbeat, and suddenly becomes doom-and-gloomy, it may be time to switch to another medication.

- Trouble falling asleep. Although insomnia is a fairly common problem among children with ADHD, if your child's medication makes things even worse, ask your physician to adjust or reduce the dosage, or to time it right before bedtime, prescribe ADHD medications with sedating qualities right before bedtime, or prescribe a sleep aid to help your child fall asleep and stay asleep.

- Rebound effects. The majority of children who take stimulants experience "rebound" effects of moodiness, irritability, and restlessness as the level of medication in the bloodstream decreases. Ask your doctor about ways to stabilize the level of medication in your child's body to avoid these annoying fluctuations.

- Appetite and weight loss. Many medications for childhood ADHD cause a reduction in appetite and subsequent weight loss. If your child is already overweight, this can be a plus. If not, ask your doctor about timing doses so your child's medication doesn't ruin her appetite for meals. If your child is losing weight despite all your best efforts, consider consulting with a registered dietitian or nutritionist. She can develop a nutrient-dense, high-calorie meal plan that will help your child maintain a healthy weight without overeating sugar and trans fats.

- Aches, pains, and tics. In some children, ADHD medications can trigger nausea, indigestion, and headaches. To ward off stomachaches, have your child take her medication with meals. If your child has ADHD as well as a coexisting condition such as Tourette's syndrome, and medication worsens her tics and muscle twitches, call your doctor.

○ Rashes and skin disturbances. Many children are allergic to the dyes and even the cellulose fillers in pills and react by breaking out in a rash. To avoid future rashes, have your physician switch your child to a medication that doesn't have the offending culprit.

○ Rapid heartbeat or increased blood pressure. If your child complains that her heart is racing, she can't catch her breath, she's experience chest pains, or if her usual exercise regime suddenly feels a lot more difficult, it may be a sign that she's taking too much medication.

SIDE EFFECTS AREN'T A LIFE SENTENCE

If side effects are seriously interfering with your child's life, make sure she understands that she won't be stuck with them for life. There are many alternatives and "fixes," from changing medication and dosage to taking a drug holiday and giving it a try later.

You may also consider consulting with other medical experts to get a fresh point of view about medications and treatments you haven't yet tried.

The good news is that side effects associated with childhood ADHD medications tend to be mild and temporary. Most of them can be eliminated by simply changing the dosage, dosage schedule, or by switching to a new medication. The even better news is that in many cases, negative side effects simply go away in a few weeks' time.

THE FINE PRINT

It's also essential to read and understand the fine print concerning your child's ADHD medication, including information regarding its half-life and peak time, how many doses your child needs to take, if the medication is short-acting or long-acting, and if the medication is available in extended-release forms so your child can take it once and forget about it for the rest of the day.

Tracking Progress

Although monitoring the effectiveness of your child's medication will require some effort on your part, the results are well worth it. By keeping track of how well the drug works over time, you and your doctor can make the necessary adjustments in medications and dosages.

To maximize the effectiveness of your child's medication and to minimize the side effects and risks, follow these easy guidelines for safe use:

O Do your homework. Find out everything you can about the ADHD medication your doctor is prescribing for your child, including potential side effects, how often to take it, special warnings, and other medications and substances that should be avoided or used with caution, including over-the-counter cold and flu remedies containing ephedrine, over-the-counter and prescription weight-loss drugs, sleep medications, decongestants, steroids, and asthma medications containing albuterol or theophylline.

O Make sure your child takes his medication as directed. He should never take more or less, or take it at a different time than prescribed by your physician.

O Don't let a high-fat breakfast sabotage your child's medication. If your child is taking certain stimulant drugs, including Adderall, Metadate, or Ritalin, a high-fat breakfast can compromise its effectiveness by delaying the drug's absorption. Instead of the drug working within the usual twenty to thirty minutes, it could take one to two hours. Rather than serving your child a high-fat breakfast such as bacon and eggs, serve him a low-fat option such as oatmeal with berries.

O Time your child's intake of foods and supplements high in vitamin C. Fruit juices high in ascorbic acid/vitamin C or citric acid (orange, grapefruit, and other drinks supplemented with vitamin C) may interfere with the absorption of Ritalin because citric acid breaks down the medication before it has a chance to be absorbed by the body. For this reason, your doctor may recommend your child avoid fruit juices as well as high-vitamin cereals and multivitamin supplements an hour before and after taking medication.

- Be patient. Finding the right medication and dose is a trial-and-error process. It will take some experimenting, as well as open, honest communication with your child's doctor, before you find the medication(s) that works best in alleviating symptoms in your child.

- Don't let your child stop a drug cold-turkey because it is ineffective or has unpleasant side effects. Your child could suffer from discontinuation syndrome, which is characterized by depression, irritability, fatigue, insomnia, and headaches that could linger for weeks or months.

MEDICATION LOGS

Keep records of how the medication is affecting your child's emotions, behavior, attention, sleep, appetite, weight, etc. Keep track of any unusual or new side effects that occur, and keep an ongoing record of how effective the medication seems to be at alleviating your child's symptoms.

You may also want to invest in a commercial medication log. For more information about purchasing a medical log, go to *www.information-logs.com*.

JUST ONE PART OF TREATMENT

Remember that medication is just one leg of your child's treatment triangle. Recording reactions to drugs on a regular basis will make it easier to isolate unusual emotional, mental, and physical symptoms that appear to be linked to medication. This will also help you identify persisting symptoms that may benefit from other types of treatment, such as cognitive or support psychotherapy, coaching, and support groups.

When Your Child's Medication Doesn't Work or Stops Working

Telltale signs that your child's medication isn't working, has stopped working, or the dosage needs to be fine-tuned include anxiousness, depression, jittery or restless feelings, being unable to sleep, new symptoms your child never experienced before, and experiencing inexplicable mood swings that seem to worsen, no matter what your child does.

Don't assume that just because your child is feeling better, she can afford to take less medication, or, conversely, that taking more medication will make your child feel even better.

There's a very small difference between the right dose and too little or too much medication, so avoid the temptation to experiment on your own. Include your doctor in your plans, and discuss your experience with him.

Important Points to Consider

Putting your child on medication can be a difficult decision. Here are a few tips to keep in mind during the process:

1. When gathering information about medication, be sure your child's doctor is able to answer all your questions about the range of options and the scientific evidence for alternative, complementary, and traditional medications. When making a decision, avoid making your decision based on your opinions about "alternative vs. traditional medicine" and think about making your decision based on medication effectiveness and safety. Educating yourself about your range of options and the pros and cons will help you make an informed choice in collaboration with your child's doctor.

2. Keeping track of your child's medication and how it is affecting her will help you and your child's doctor evaluate her progress. You'll also be able to tell when something feels "off" about your child.

3. When you see positive results from your child's medication, be sure to write them down. It may even help to point them out to your child.

4. It might take time to find the right medication for your child. Trial and error is not uncommon. Try not to get discouraged. When you feel yourself getting overwhelmed, take a step back and remind yourself you are doing the best you can.

5. Do your research. Take time to understand medication options for your child. Being prepared for potential side effects or negative responses to the medication can help you evaluate the effectiveness of the treatment rationally.

 **CHAPTER 14**

The Role of Behavior Modification Therapy

Trying to get children diagnosed with ADHD to behave at home and school is the biggest challenge parents confront. Even when using conscious parenting techniques, you may find that your child's behavior does not improve or worsens. Aggressive youngsters become increasingly alienated, defiant, and antisocial with each passing year. Compliant children become more upset, depressed, and self-destructive. It is important not to abandon your conscious parenting techniques in the face of difficulty. In fact, this is the time when you will need these skills the most. Before you react hastily, give yourself some time to re-evaluate the treatment options you and your child can try next. A behavior modification program may provide the solution your family needs.

Origin of Behavior Modification

Behavior modification is based on a number of different theories and research studies. It was influenced by the conditioning principles set forth by Russian physiologist Ivan Pavlov, theories set forth by American psychologist B.F. Skinner, and the work of South African psychiatrist Joseph Wolpe.

Ivan Pavlov was most famous for training dogs to salivate at the sound of a bell—a case of rewarding and shaping behavior that usually cannot be deliberately controlled. Pavlov demonstrated how such responses can be learned and also can be suppressed. This has implications for treating emotional reactions.

Skinner was a pioneer in the field of operant conditioning, which believes that behavior generally understood as conscious and intentional is modified by its consequences. Consciousness was considered to be relatively unimportant in the control of behavior. Joseph Wolpe, a pioneer in applying these results to therapy, was famous for his pioneering efforts in the areas of desensitization and assertiveness training. By the 1970s, behavior therapy was widely used in treating a variety of mental conditions, including depression, anxiety, phobias, and ADHD.

Because behavior modification is often used to treat teens with eating disorders and drug abuse, behavior modification may help your child reduce symptoms of both ADHD as well as one of these coexisting conditions. Behavior modification is most effective when used in combination with ADHD medications and psychotherapy.

What Is Behavior Modification?

By systematically rewarding selected behavior in a consistent, highly organized fashion and ignoring undesirable behavior, trainers teach animals to perform amazing feats. They teach dolphins and lions to jump through hoops. Pigeons learn to carry messages to distant locations. Seeing-eye dogs master the art of guiding the blind about town without becoming distracted by passing cars, animals, and crowds. In short, animals learn to respond in ways most people never would have thought possible.

Psychologists have long recognized that the same straightforward principles and simple procedures work well for animals of all kinds, from human beings to fruit flies. Behavior modification programs are effective for helping children and adults alike eliminate troublesome behavior, break destructive habits, develop better self-control, and respond in healthier ways.

Types of Behavior Modification

Every behavior modification program is different because it is tailored to a specific child. In general there are two basic types:

○ Behavior modification (traditional)

○ Cognitive-behavior therapy

The secret to a successful behavior modification program is to define small, readily obtainable goals and systematically reward each small accomplishment until new habits are formed. Children must be set up to succeed. Failure results when the tasks are too difficult or the rewards insufficiently motivating or delayed.

GETTING GOOD RESULTS

Impressive results are commonplace when trained professionals conduct modification programs in controlled environments. When scientists methodically follow carefully designed protocols in laboratories and special education teachers work with students in self-contained classrooms, they typically get excellent results.

WHY RESULTS CAN BE POOR

When ordinary parents and teachers try to carry out behavior programs at home and school, the results often prove very disappointing. Many parents are sure that behavior modification won't work for their children, because their past attempts to solve behavior problems by doling out rewards and imposing punishment followed a predictable pattern: Most everything they tried worked for a time, but nothing worked for long.

Although parents typically conclude that failure means that their youngsters are especially difficult, strong-willed, defiant, or resistant, the real problem usually lies elsewhere. The success of a behavior modification program depends on the adult properly applying the techniques involved, not on how the child responds.

Using rewards to control behavior need not feel coercive because both parents and children enjoy increased satisfaction with one another. Behavior modification has been shown to reverse negative communication patterns and strengthen the parent-child relationship.

Creating and maintaining a behavior modification program is often too complex for many parents. Working with a professional trained and experienced in the specific area of behavior therapy will make it easier for you to create and maintain an effective program.

How Behavior Modification Works

Although successful behavior modifications differ from child to child, they all incorporate the following ten basic principles:

1. Rewards are given immediately for good behavior.

2. Because immediacy and frequency are essential, a number of small rewards, such as stickers, can be cashed in for bigger, more distant rewards.

3. Rewards need to be things the child desires and does not get in other ways.

4. Rewards are not withheld because a parent is angry with the child.

5. Rewards are never taken away after a child has earned them.

6. Children should be praised for their successes.

7. Children should receive unconditional love from parents regardless of how well they perform in the behavior modification program.

8. Desired behavior should be broken into steps small enough to allow your child to succeed almost every time.

9. Parents should be cautious with punishments. If used, they should be immediate and short-term.

10. If the behavior system is not working, the child should never be blamed. Because behavior modification is a highly sophisticated technique, it should be developed and adapted by a trained professional.

Helping Your Therapist Develop a Customized Program for Your Child

The first step in developing a behavior modification program is to create a list of the behaviors you want to eliminate or to increase. Examples of behaviors to eliminate may be interrupting when someone else is speaking or arguing when told to do homework. Examples of behaviors to increase might include getting dressed in time to go to school, being in bed by 9 P.M., and remaining seated during dinner.

Behaviors that are general, vague, or subject to interpretation such as "don't be rude" must be rewritten so that they reflect specific, concrete, observable actions, such as, "Use appropriate language," and "Ask to borrow things first." Goals should be the positive opposite of a negative behavior. So instead of "Don't slam your door" you would use "Close your door quietly" so you teach a child the expected behavior.

Similarly, internal states of mind and attitudes such as "don't be so argumentative" must be rewritten as specific behaviors such as "do homework when instructed without arguing."

IMPORTANCE OF DEFINING BEHAVIOR

Defining behavior precisely is a must. Saying that you expect your child to be polite when relatives are visiting really does not tell your youngster what to do. Is she to preface her answers with "yes, sir," "no, ma'am," and "I'm not sure," instead of mumbling, "yeah," "naw," and "I dunno"? Should she say "please" when she wants a snack, "thank you" when given a present, and "excuse me" before interrupting a conversation? Or would you just be happy if she would refrain from punching her little cousin, using the sofa as a trampoline, or asking the company to go home so she can watch television?

Parents often think that their child knows how to behave properly and is simply being stubborn, lazy, or defiant. Time and again it turns out that the youngster truly does not understand that when mother says, "do the dishes," she also means "put away the food, wipe the table and counters, and carry out the trash."

CREATING TARGET BEHAVIORS TO MODIFY

After creating a list of target behaviors to modify, try to eliminate the negatives and replace them with positives by changing the "don'ts" to "dos." Saying that your daughter is not to hit her little brother does not explain what she should do when he takes her toys or taunts her. Telling her to ignore a tormentor may not be realistic and doesn't teach her how to set limits and defend herself.

Importance of Rewarding Good Behavior

Children tend to repeat behavior that is consistently followed by positive consequences. Behavior modification programs use rewards to reinforce desirable behavior. There are two types of rewards: material rewards and social rewards.

Material rewards include toys, treats, outings, privileges, and permissions. Social rewards include hugs, smiles, compliments, and kudos.

For a behavior modification program to succeed, you must reward your child step by small step for a few simple things he can readily accomplish. Then you must reward him every single time at first, though with care the frequency of rewards might be reduced later.

It is best to work with no more than one or two simple behaviors at a time. When the desired behavior is inculcated, then another one may be selected until your child has thoroughly mastered them, before presenting him with more challenging tasks.

Because you will be providing many rewards each day, material rewards must necessarily be inexpensive. Items such as stickers, marbles, or trading cards appeal to some children. Many parents give a piece of candy. This can be very effective, though it may not be wise to give too much candy to children.

It is important to use rewards the child actually wants, and it is generally a good idea to reserve those specific rewards for the behavior modification program so that the child does not become satiated with them by getting them in other ways. If a child loses interest in a reward, a new reward should be used.

Older children and teenagers may be able to work on a "point system" in which rewards are given in point values that they can redeem for access to privileges. You can create a "privilege menu" together for how many points are earned for each behavior and how many are required for each privilege

CHAINING

"Chaining" is a technique for rewarding less pleasurable behavior with more pleasurable behavior. The most aversive behavior comes first. For some children it might be getting dressed in the morning. Using a chaining approach, dressing is the first thing the child would do.

Brushing her teeth might be less of an issue, and might come next. Getting herself out the door on time might be rewarded with a special treat to take along to school. Keep in mind though, that any one of these steps might need a specific reward as the program is being developed.

Small, immediate rewards should be tallied up for major and more distant rewards. Immediate rewards might be getting to play a video game for twenty minutes, being allowed to choose the restaurant when the family eats out, or deciding which movie the family watches. Outings such as a trip to the mall, city park, or library are popular, distant rewards.

ROLE OF SOCIAL REWARDS

Social rewards are interactions that your child enjoys and that are affirming. They can be smiles, hugs, pats on the back, the thumbs-up sign, praise, expressions of appreciation, positive acknowledgment, overhearing glowing comments, and spending pleasant time with a parent.

Pleasant time can include playing ball, making brownies, planting a garden, reading a bedtime story together, going to the park together, etc. When asked, children usually choose material rewards over social rewards, but social rewards are powerful and important. They are more meaningful to most children in the long run. However, a reward is only effective if it is motivating. For this reason, material rewards are often effective, even when they are not considered to be ideal.

ROLE OF PHYSICAL REWARDS

Make it a habit to administer verbal or physical pats on the back whenever you give your youngster a material reward. Some children are indifferent to praise, smiles, and kudos because every other sentence their parents utter is "good job!" until it sounds like a verbal tic. Youngsters come to regard such glowing comments for what they are: meaningless and empty. At the same time, everyone needs unconditional positive regard. Children should not be deprived of generalized affection.

IMPORTANCE OF IMMEDIATE REWARDS

Because rewards must be given immediately after a desired behavior occurs, it is usually more efficient to give tokens or other small prizes or treats, for example colorful stickers that can be traded for a bigger prize later.

As anyone who has tried to diet knows, it is hard to remain motivated to work toward a far-off goal. In most cases reward systems only work when children feel rewarded immediately. If you discover that your child is not motivated by certain rewards, change them. If she cannot readily earn rewards, make them easier to reach.

YOUR CHILD'S ROLE IN A BEHAVIOR MODIFICATION PROGRAM

Children should be involved in all phases of a behavior modification program. Their help determining what rewards they can earn and what they must do to get them is important.

Solicit your child's input before deciding how many stickers she needs to accumulate in order to earn a trip to the skating rink or to get a new toy. She must view the rewards as worthwhile and believe she can earn them for a behavior modification program to work.

Explain that you are going to begin rewarding her for good behavior and help her brainstorm a long list of the toys, treats, outings, privileges, and permissions that she would like. Record all of her wishes. You may not be willing to fulfill her heart's desire for a horse by moving Black Beauty into your backyard. But learning that horses mean that much to her may provide clues to highly motivating rewards. You might consider providing stickers with pictures of horses for her to affix to a chart, watching *The Black Stallion* video, driving to the country so she can pat a horse, letting her take a riding lesson at a stable, going to see a rodeo or horse show, transferring a picture of a horse onto her T-shirt, riding a pony at an amusement park, and helping her arrange to work at a stable.

Increasing the Chances of Success

To increase the chance of success in a behavior modification program, even very small rewards such as tokens and stickers should not be taken away once earned—even if the child does something displeasing or wrong. Remember that children are not at fault when a behavior modification program falters.

Tell your child you love him often, and be affectionate regardless of the progress of the behavior modification program. Children who feel unloved are likely to become depressed, angry, and rebellious.

In the context of the behavior modification program, praise specific achievements. And when you do, provide a detailed description of the behavior you like: "I'm impressed that you remembered to ask your brother to pass the salt instead of reaching across the table."

Combining material and social rewards is especially powerful. Trainers provide material rewards such as scraps of meat to puppies at the outset of training. With the combination of praise and pats and the food, dogs soon learn to associate the two. Once they make the association, praise alone serves as a reward and keeps their behavior on track. Similarly, children eventually associate the positive feelings about material rewards with their parents' smiles and expressions of pleasure. In time, approval is enough to keep them going.

CREATING DESIRABLE BEHAVIORS

Because a youngster sometimes manages to control his temper or clean his room doesn't mean that he can do either easily. If your child quickly loses interest in earning rewards, you are asking too much of him.

Behavior modification programs work because they set children up to succeed. To do that, you must break each target behavior into a series of small tasks that your child can easily manage and which are rewarded immediately. Each small success builds confidence and creates the can-do attitude that motivates children to tackle new challenges.

DEFINING TASKS

Perhaps you want your youngster to clean his room without an argument, but his usual response when told to turn off the television and get started is to ignore you. If you turn off the television and firmly tell him to clean his room, he has a fit and promises to clean it later, but later never comes. Or, he goes to his room but does not work.

To solve this problem with a behavior modification program, the first step is to get him to respond when you speak to him, whether he is busy doing something else or is purposely ignoring you. Inform him of this goal, write it on his behavior chart, and specify the reward or the number of tokens he can earn each time he achieves it. Then, when you want to speak with him, go to the room where he is playing, say his name in a normal tone of voice or gently touch his shoulder, and then reward him when he looks up, even if he only glances your way by chance. As you hand him a token, sticker, or another predetermined reward, say, "I appreciate your stopping what you're doing when I need to talk with you. Thanks." After he has been reinforced a number of times in this way, he'll be better at noticing that you are speaking to him.

After your child is consistently responding, compliment him on his accomplishment and announce that he is ready for the next challenge, which might be to accompany you to his bedroom without protest when it is time to clean his room.

Describe the rewards he will earn for each success. Then, if he willingly accompanies you to the bedroom, reward him even if he doesn't clean up his room. Help him pick up toys or clothing, or pick up for him, and reassure him that he will be able to handle that task in time. Don't advance to the next step until he can consistently walk with you to the bedroom and refrain from arguing. When you are sure he has mastered that challenge, describe the next goal: He will pick up his clothes from the floor and put them in the laundry.

THE ROLE OF PUNISHMENT

Punishment involves following an undesired behavior with an aversive stimulus that is calculated to suppress that behavior in the future. This could involve taking away an enjoyable activity such as watching television or playing video games.

In a behavior therapy context, punishments, if any, are defined in advance in working with your child, just as are rewards. They are never arbitrary or unexpected. A punishment in the behavior therapy context is a brief, predefined event administered in a preplanned manner in response to a specific behavior. It is part of the behavior therapy plan, just as are rewards.

Punishment is often not very effective in the long run for children with ADHD. Use it with caution, keep punishments brief, and administer them to your child in a private setting to avoid embarrassing your child. Instead of taking away a child's access to television for a week after she's done something wrong, take it away for a half-hour each time.

Ask your child's opinion before deciding what the penalty should be for a particular type of misbehavior, and then watch carefully to see if losing privileges really deters misbehavior and motivates your child to behave better.

THE ROLE OF EXTINCTION

Extinction involves eliminating something that rewards an undesired behavior so that it will stop occurring. When the reward is eliminated, the frequency of the behavior may increase at first, but it will then drop off to near zero because the consequence that keeps it going has been removed.

Most children find attention to be rewarding. Frequently, if annoying behaviors that are reinforced by attention are ignored, they will at first increase in strength or frequency and then drop off within a few days. This happens because the behaviors are no longer rewarded with attention. Nagging is an example of a behavior that may be reduced in this way.

Many youngsters misbehave in order to get a reaction from their parents. Even negative attention is better than no attention, so being scolded can actually be more rewarding than being ignored. Ignoring negative behavior is an example of using extinction.

Many children simply do not know how to get positive attention. Their parents ignore them when they are playing quietly, refuse invitations to play board games, and decline requests to go outside to toss a football. These parents are chronically stressed and exhausted and only find the wherewithal to respond when a behavior problem compels them to get involved. Behavior modification programs often succeed simply because parents are forced to notice and respond to their child's good behavior.

Overcoming Challenges in Behavior Modification

There are some limits on what can be taught using behavior modification. You must be realistic when targeting behavior you want to change. It is doubtful that you can turn your shy, artistic bookworm into a football star. At the same time, do not underestimate how much your child can ultimately achieve.

THE CHALLENGES OF SUSTAINING NEW BEHAVIOR

Learners usually understand what they are to do and should be able to earn rewards in short order. Being able to sustain their new behavior over time is more challenging, but the positive feelings and consequences the new behavior spurs can help.

Most people can diet or stop smoking for a day or two, but continuing to abstain from fat and cigarettes gets harder rather than easier as time passes. That's because the strain of behaving in unfamiliar ways wears them down. Similarly, although a hyperactive youngster may be capable of sitting still for five minutes at a stretch, doing so requires a tremendous effort.

Until your child finds a way to calm her behavior, she may well feel as if her nerves are on edge, screaming for her to move about. Your child is likely to require changes in rewards to stay motivated. New behavior should come to reinforce itself through improved quality of life and interpersonal relations.

Stress from another problem or difficulty that happens to arise while a behavior modification program is in progress can readily cause a setback. Reverting to old behavior patterns does not mean that no progress has been made. Until new habits develop, lapses are to be expected.

IMPORTANCE OF CONTINUED REWARDS

Do not hold back from giving a reward because your child is playing quietly or is busily doing homework for fear your interruption will create a distraction and end your precious moments of peace. Otherwise, you will quickly revert to the same destructive patterns of nagging your youngster when she does something wrong instead of rewarding her for good behavior, and progress will stall. In time, you may be able to reduce the frequency of rewards.

Until rewarding your youngster for virtually every positive behavior as you have planned becomes a habit, remaining consistent is not easy. Be patient with yourself, and reward yourself for your successes at carrying out the program. What you must do to succeed is to modify some of your behavior—perhaps the very same behavior you are trying to get your child to embrace.

BE PATIENT

If it takes an entire month for your child to pick up her dirty clothes each evening without an argument, don't get discouraged. Many parents of children diagnosed with ADHD have to yell to get their attention for years on end. Many adults are too undisciplined to put their dirty clothes in the laundry each day, and the result is arguments with roommates and marital strife. Do not underestimate the importance of small accomplishments.

> Children with ADHD have sluggish reward circuits in their brains that make otherwise interesting tasks seem dull and dull tasks seem unbearable. Growing their interest by increasing the magnitude of reward, you are helping them be successful at completing tasks, which will give them confidence and independence.

Role of Cognitive-Behavior Therapy

Traditional behavior modification uses the consistent use of rewards and consequences to encourage children to behave in a positive way and discourage them from behaving in a negative way. Cognitive-behavior therapy is similar but different. Instead of rewards and consequences, it uses a systematic approach to changing the way your child thinks and acts by using conditioning and association.

This therapy is called *cognitive* because it attempts to determine what your child's dialogue and thought patterns are and how they relate to his behavior and moods. It's called *behavior* because it uses conditioned responses to your child's internal dialogues to change his behavior.

Your child will work with a therapist to determine his problem behaviors and he and the therapist will determine ways to correct them.

First, the therapist looks at one behavior at a time to try to determine the child's motivations and reasons for acting that way. Next, your child and therapist will look at where and when your child exhibits this behavior, looking at your child's motivations (or feelings and thoughts) for acting that way, and when the behavior typically occurs, or in what circumstances.

After the therapist and child have a handle on when a behavior occurs and why, they begin to look for ways to change your child's behavior. Once your child is armed with these strategies, he can use them whenever he is tempted to repeat the behavior.

Although children can't usually stop a negative behavior the first time with the first strategy they and their therapist come up with, in time, they can make adjustments until they end up with a strategy that works.

Combining Medication with Behavior Modification

As noted in Chapter 13, a landmark study that researched the most effective treatments for children with ADHD showed that children who used both medication and behavior modification saw a decrease in symptoms and were able to lower their daily doses of medication. Children who just took medication were not able to.

The study also showed that children who received both types of treatment saw a larger decrease in inattention, hyperactivity, and impulsivity than children who received just medication, although children who received just medication enjoyed fewer symptoms than children who just received behavior modification.

The study also noted that although medication was better than behavior modification at reducing hyperactivity, inattention, and impulsivity, it had no effect on the oppositional defiant behavior that sometimes accompanies ADHD, children's relationships with their classmates and peers, and their academic achievement.

Important Points to Consider

Trying any new treatment for your child's ADHD can be scary. Remember that positive results may not happen immediately. Don't get discouraged!

1. Simple changes such as altering your language can modify how your child behaves. Be specific with your desires.

2. If you see your child exhibiting inappropriate behavior, instead of just telling him not to do that behavior, tell him what he should do instead. Remember to stay calm—reacting with anger never helps.

3. Using rewards for behavior modification can be just as enjoyable for you as for your child. Maybe your child's reward for behaving well is an extra story at bedtime. This means more quality parenting time for you!

4. Never underestimate the power of praise.

5. Punishing your child can be difficult, but you don't have to lose your cool. When you feel yourself getting angry, give yourself a few minutes of alone time to calm down before talking to your child about her punishment.

 **CHAPTER 15**

The Benefits of Talk Therapy

Although medications for treating childhood ADHD have proven to be very successful in reducing symptoms, they can't teach new skills or improve the organizational and interpersonal challenges that typically accompany the disorder. Talk therapy takes many forms but always involves talking with a trained therapist. Depending on the specific type of talk therapy, your child or teen will learn about the neurobiological natures of the disorder, stop blaming herself, and develop new tools and strategies for coping with everyday symptoms at school, at home, and with friends. Although building trust with a stranger can be difficult for any child, encourage your child to be honest with her therapist from the beginning. Be supportive, and don't expect change to occur immediately. Understand that you are giving your child tools that will help her better herself now and in the future.

Anatomy of Talk Therapy

Basically, talk therapy is exactly what it sounds like: Your child sits down with a therapist and talks about something she wants to correct, or get over, or forgive.

There are several different types of talk therapy. They include insight-oriented therapy, which aims to help your child understand what she does and why; supportive therapy, where your child gets the support and encouragement she may need to deal with her symptoms; skills training, where she learns specific skills that may be lacking and causing her problems in school; and psycho-educational counseling, where your child learns about the various aspects of ADHD and strategies to cope with them.

Many children benefit from group counseling, where they work with other children with similar issues; relationships therapy, where they work on skills necessary to make and keep friends; and family therapy, where the entire family gets together to address issues and problems related to ADHD.

Some children also use ADHD coaches to develop and strengthen organizational and time-management skills. For more information on cognitive-behavior therapy—another type of talk therapy where your child learns to change the way she thinks and acts using conditioning and association—see Chapter 14.

Why and When Talk Therapy Works

Everyone in life needs someone to talk to, whether you are going through a major life challenge like childhood ADHD, or just trying to figure out how to cope with a minor setback.

Children with ADHD have myriad issues to contend with, from the symptoms of the disorder to the fact that ADHD is often an isolating syndrome that turns its victims into social outcasts.

From learning about causes and treatments to finding new ways to coexist happily and healthily with the disorder so your child is exercising his innate strengths and playing down his shortcomings, psychotherapy gives your child the coping skills, strategies, and skills he needs to live with ADHD.

It's important to remember that childhood ADHD has no ultimate cure. Neither medication nor psychotherapy can completely eliminate the symptoms, however, psychotherapy can help you and your child understand, manage, and minimize symptoms so they are less likely to have a negative impact on your child's life.

Which Talk Therapy Is Right for Your Child?

Just as there are many different regimens for weight loss, there are many different types of therapy. Some focus on helping your child come to a better understanding of why she thinks, acts, and feels differently than "normal" people. Others help your child adjust her behavior, emotions, and thinking so they don't sabotage her personal relationships, her ability to perform in school, get into college, or use her unique talent productively.

LEARNING THROUGH PSYCHO-EDUCATION

If your child has never been in therapy before and has just been diagnosed with ADHD, psycho-education therapy is often a good place to start. In this type of therapy the therapist acts more as an instructor than a therapist to teach you and your child about the disorder.

In psycho-education, you and your child will learn that symptoms you might have thought were your child's fault, or that you assumed were caused by your child's innate laziness, lack of motivation, or disinterest, are actually the result of a neurobiological imbalance of neurotransmitters that control attention and impulse.

You'll also learn why it's harder for your child than others to pay attention, focus, remember things, get things done on time, start things, prioritize, and know when to shift gears.

Learning and understanding the biological roots of childhood ADHD can also help you and your child begin to banish years of guilt and blame, and open the floodgates for seeking the help your child needs to overcome symptoms.

SKILLS TRAINING THERAPY

Children with ADHD often feel disordered and as though their lives are spiraling out of control. In order to compensate for their symptoms, they develop idiosyncratic and often ineffective ways of dealing with school and home-related tasks. Another type of therapy, or skills training, helps children with ADHD develop the executive skills they need to function more effectively at school.

Disorganization is one of the biggest problems facing children with ADHD. If your child can start projects but can't complete them because she misplaces important documents, a skills training therapist can provide the hands-on help your child needs to get and keep her schoolwork in order.

Skills training helps replace inefficient habits with more effective ones. It also teaches children with ADHD how to enhance their organizational skills through the use of time-management skills, audio and visual cues, electronic organizers, date books, calendars, and lists. It offers ways to structure tasks to help your child feel more competent and accomplished.

If your child has concurrent learning difficulties as well as organizational and executive functioning skill deficits, an educational therapist might be a good choice for a provider. Educational therapists are trained in academic remediation as well as teaching your child strategies for coping with ADHD. The Association of Educational Therapists' website is a good place to start to locate an educational therapist in your area. Go to *www.aetonline.org*.

Insight Therapy

Talk therapy can take many different forms, including insight therapy, support therapy, and group therapy. In insight therapy, your child examines the past for "ah-ha" moments.

The underlying premise of insight therapy is that actions are the result of many conscious and unconscious factors, some of which may stem back to childhood experiences he has completely forgotten on a conscious level, but still reacts to on an emotional level. The goal of insight therapy is to uncover the motivating factors behind what your child does, and find ways to adjust them to result in better outcomes.

Insight therapy isn't always a walk in the park. Often, delving into the past to try to figure out present behavior can uncover thoughts, emotions, and memories your child or teen may have suppressed because they were too painful to remember. A trained therapist can help your child deal with painful recollections, and find ways to assist your child in learning and growing from them.

Children with ADHD often have highly creative minds that are adept at brainstorming ideas—not to mention coming up with excuses. Without a trained therapist to help your child cut through the maze, he might never figure out why he routinely "forgets" to do his homework.

Fortunately, an insight therapist is trained to listen closely and carefully to your child's real and fabricated problems and excuses, and can help him untangle them so he can come up with a solution to a problem before it has a negative impact on his life.

It could be as easy as making sure all his homework materials are in one place so he can find them and get his homework done promptly, or putting visual cues on his computer to remind him when a project is due.

Your therapist may not always be able to help your child correct or eliminate the problem at hand, but he will probably be able to help your child arrive at a compromise that he can tolerate and live with.

Support Therapy

If an insight therapist serves as a detective to help your child uncover and understand unconscious motives, a support therapist acts more like your child's personal cheerleader. After years of living with the disappointment, rejection, and failure, your child may feel like she needs someone to help her pick herself up and dust herself off.

REPLACING NEGATIVES WITH POSITIVES

Many children with ADHD are also mired in negative, gloom-and-doom thinking, primarily because they've spent a large part of their lives internalizing years of criticism hurled their way because of their ADHD symptoms.

If your child is one of them, a support therapist can help your child replace negative thoughts, self-criticism, and low self-esteem with strategies that lead to more positive thinking.

Support therapy requires time and patience on the part of your child and her therapist. Your child didn't become negative overnight, and she's not going to emerge from her therapist's office with a positive, radiant glow until she's learned how to stop her negative self-thinking in its tracks, and replace it with self-affirming thoughts and feelings.

TIME-HONORED STRATEGIES

Here are some tried-and-true strategies support therapists use to help children derail negative thoughts and self-image:

O Encourage your child to catch herself in the act. The minute she starts thinking something negative about herself, tell her to imagine it's a monster dragging her down to the pits. Or have her try to "catch" her negative thoughts by imagining them in a thought bubble. The first step is to become more aware of her negative thoughts so she can help gain the upper hand.

- Encourage your child to stop playing that broken record in her head. When your child repeatedly tells herself "basic truths" she believes about herself, such as, "I'm too dumb to pass this test," or "I always screw things up on a date," the limiting self-talk can make her give up before she even tries. Your therapist can help your child practice saying affirmative things to herself that are probably a lot truer than those old, negative songs that have been on autoplay for years.

- Help your child get some perspective. Another problem children with ADHD experience is a tendency to magnify their own shortcomings. Maybe your child always thinks she's to blame, no matter what the situation, or she emphasizes the negatives and eliminates the positive when it comes to her past and present accomplishments. As an objective party, your therapist can give your child the reality check she needs to readjust her attitudes about herself.

- Encourage your child to learn to reframe. Just as a beautiful picture frame can enhance rather than obscure the beauty of a painting, putting a positive spin on things can turn a mistake into an opportunity for improvement. Did your child forget to turn in her homework? Instead of telling herself she's so stupid she can't remember simple things, teach her to state the obvious in a non-judgmental way: "I forgot to turn in my homework." Then have her ask herself what she can do to remember to do it tomorrow.

- Help your child get rid of the absolutes. If your child is constantly beating herself up for "always" being late, or "never" remembering important dates, have her focus on the many things in life she does right. Replaying that endless (inaccurate) record in her head that says she does "everything" wrong is the sort of negative reinforcement she needs to banish from her life.

- Encourage your child to be nice to herself. Your child with ADHD has already had her share of self-criticism and rejection. Have her work with her therapist to find ways to nurture her soul, whether it's listening to inspiring music, reading empowering books, taking a restorative walk through nature, or talking things over with a supportive friend.

○ Your child will need time and practice to improve her self-image, but once she gets the ball rolling, her positive self-talk may well become a self-fulfilling prophecy. As she gains self-confidence and self-respect, she'll make changes to improve the quality of her life, and feel better about herself in return. Your child will discover that success begets success.

Relationship Therapy

In relationship therapy, or therapy that focuses on friendships and other relationships, your child learns how to manage ADHD symptoms that may be affecting his ability to make and keep meaningful relationships, act appropriately during casual dating, feel comfortable in social settings, and work well with people on the job.

Some children with ADHD, especially hyperactive children, manifest their symptoms by jumping into conversations and situations where they're not invited, constantly interrupting others, or behaving in a hostile, arrogant, or aggressive fashion—all behaviors that tend to alienate people. Your child's therapist can teach your child effective ways to manage his impulses, such as counting to ten before speaking.

Making and keeping friends can be very difficult for children with ADHD. Because of their long history of misunderstanding others, confusing communication cues, and being unable to read and translate nonverbal cues, they are likely to withdraw from social interaction and feel more comfortable alone than with others.

FRIENDS AND CHILDREN WITH ADHD

Research shows that children with ADHD get along best with friends who are low-maintenance, who don't expect or need regular contact, and who are nonjudgmental. If your child has a friend with ADHD who has "drifted" away, ask your child to make sure he's not overestimating the friend's ability to maintain regular contact.

Because of their forgetfulness, children with ADHD may also forget about friends' needs, and fail to do the many little things required to keep a friendship going and growing. Your child's therapist can teach him the importance of calling friends on the phone, sending a friendly e-mail or text to check on them, remembering their birthdays, congratulating them, or consoling them for the death of a loved one.

REINING IN IMPULSIVE PROMISING

One problem shared by many children with ADHD is the tendency to make promises and commitments they can't keep, or which they forgot they even made. Unfortunately, the forgetfulness that makes your child's friends feel unloved or unappreciated can also make them wonder if your child is too selfish, self-centered, or narcissistic to care about anyone else's needs but his own.

Your child's therapist can work with your child on strategies that will help him check his impulses before making grandiose promises he can't keep. She can encourage your child to learn how to say "no" when someone's expectations are impossible for him to meet, and to compensate for his inherent tendency toward aloofness and solitude by making a conscious attempt to be more interested and engaged in the lives of others.

Group Counseling

In addition to the individual types of counseling discussed previously, children with ADHD often find family or group counseling very helpful. In group counseling, several people with a common issue meet together with a therapist.

Interacting with others and hearing their problems can help reduce your child's feelings of isolation and give her the support and motivation to change troublesome ways of thinking, feeling, and acting.

Many children with ADHD feel awkward in social settings. Because of their impulsivity, they also have a tendency to interrupt others, or to butt into conversations. Group therapy can provide children with ADHD with a safe place to develop and practice appropriate social skills, and to get moral support and feedback in a safe and protected setting.

Family Therapy

In family therapy, the entire family works with a counselor to help family members understand the nature of childhood ADHD and why your child thinks, acts, and feels the way he does. Family therapy helps to overcome misunderstandings regarding the disorder, change the family's patterns of blame, and guide the family to make the adjustments needed for family harmony.

Living with a child with ADHD can translate into household chaos. Therapists can help families organize the household so the child with ADHD functions more effectively on a daily basis. Therapists can also suggest ways to remove some burdens from the children who don't have ADHD so they feel more like siblings and less like parents.

IMPORTANCE OF ROUTINES

Your child's therapist can also help you and your child with ADHD create simple routines that help minimize household clutter and chaos. For instance, establishing a central location for house or car keys can help prevent them from getting lost or scattered all over the house.

Creating orderly routines may also help rein in chaos. Although people without ADHD find it easy to establish and automatically follow routines, there is no such thing as an automatic routine for many children with ADHD.

DIVIDE AND CONQUER

Divide and conquer is another effective way to relieve the burden of household chores in families with a member who has ADHD. Your therapist will help you and your child divvy up the chores so your child with ADHD is responsible for creative tasks such as cooking, gardening, and decorating, while your other children tackle chores that require more attention to detail and focus.

How to Find a Therapist

Many parents wonder how they can determine which type of therapy is best for their children. In general, psycho-education and talk therapy can help your child deal with feelings of low self-esteem, inadequacy, anxiety, depression, and feelings of underachievement. Behavior and skills training therapy are useful in helping your child develop new ways to deal with specific issues, rebuild organizational and planning skills, learn time-management skills, and learn more effective communication skills.

Working with a therapist you respect and trust, and who feels like a good match for your child, is usually more important than the type of therapy you choose. Your and your child's willingness to be a regular participant in the therapeutic process is also essential to the success of any therapy your child undergoes.

To find a good therapist in your area, talk to members of your support group, or ask your family physician or ADHD practitioners for a referral. Or contact CHADD at *www.chadd.org* for information on therapists in your area.

When you are interviewing therapists, ask if they incorporate mindfulness activities into sessions. Many therapists now teach mindfulness concepts and practice the skills in session. Parents can reinforce the techniques used out of sessions.

The Importance of ADHD Support Groups

Many children with ADHD avoid social situations and, as a result, become isolated and out of touch. Support groups can provide kids with ADHD a safe place to develop and practice social skills in a supportive, nonjudgmental, and caring environment.

By sharing their stories with others, and learning that others share the same difficulties, kids with ADHD can start to overcome the feelings of isolation that often make them feel like social outcasts. They can start to build the supportive relationships they need to carry them through challenging times. Kids can also practice appropriate behavior.

LEARNING THE GROUND RULES

Your child will get the best support from his group if he knows the ground rules going in, and understands that being part of a support group entails listening as well as talking. It's also very important that your child understand the structure of his support group and how it functions. Some groups combine casual socializing with group sharing during the meeting, others set aside opportunities to socialize and mingle before and/or after the official meeting.

Your child should understand that an ADHD support group isn't an excuse to "let it all hang out," but an opportunity to share mutual problems and build on his social skills in a supportive setting. He should check that his impulsivity doesn't cause him to chatter away without thinking and self-censoring, or that his hyperactivity doesn't cause him to jump into conversations before he's invited.

LEARNING PROPER ETIQUETTE

When your child first joins a support group, encourage him to test the waters before taking the plunge. Suggest that he sit quietly and observe for the first few meetings before actively participating. Make sure he understands that sharing too much about himself may make him feel uncomfortable later, whereas sharing too little may make him seem indifferent or bored to others in the group.

Proper support group etiquette involves taking cues from others to find the right balance between talking and listening. A good rule of thumb for your child to follow is to listen more than he talks, and contribute only when he has something concrete and appropriate to say.

By joining a support group, your child has made an unwritten agreement to listen as well as talk, and to view the support group as a tool for helping himself as well as others to gain insight and find solutions to ADHD-related challenges and problems.

Important Points to Consider

You can help your child get the most out of her therapy by remembering a few simple tips:

1. Therapy can be draining at any age, especially for a child. Be patient with your child and his progress.

2. You can help your child outside of therapy by encouraging her to identify negative thoughts and feelings in the moment.

3. Remind your child that everyone makes mistakes, and that the best way to move forward is to admit his mistake, decide what he could have done differently, and then let it go.

4. Just as you encourage your child to be kind to others, encourage her to be kind to herself. Don't forget to be kind to yourself as well.

5. Just as your child needs support to handle her ADHD symptoms, you need support to continue helping her. Look for ADHD support groups, and confide in a trusted friend about the various struggles you are facing.

 **CHAPTER 16**

Finding the Silver Lining

The three major symptoms of childhood ADHD—hyperactivity, impulsivity, and inattention—create many challenges for children who suffer from the disorder. These include problems performing at school, difficulty making and keeping relationships, and an inability to function comfortably or appropriately in social settings. But these symptoms may also have a silver lining. Hyperactivity can give your child the energy she needs to work longer and harder; impulsivity can provide the courage and drive your child needs to take great leaps of faith; and inattention can make it easier for your child to move between projects. Not only can conscious parenting techniques help you cope with the difficulties you and your family face, but they can also help you identify the positive qualities your child has. By employing mindfulness and emotional awareness in your everyday life, you can learn to refocus your attention on the positive instead of the negative.

Counting Your Blessings

As discussed in previous chapters, childhood ADHD doesn't have to be a curse for life. Many famous inventors, scientists, writers, movie stars, filmmakers, artists, musicians, rocket scientists, politicians, and others have used their unique ADHD strengths to carve out permanent places in history.

In fact, as researchers discover more and more about the disorder, they are redefining what it means to be a child with ADHD—not just a group of negative attributes, but a group of positive traits as well.

Scientists believe that one reason children with ADHD may excel at creative tasks is that their brains are wired in a way that limits inhibition. A child with ADHD may find it easier to follow the beat of his own drummer than children without ADHD, who feel compelled to conform to societal norms.

The Hidden Gifts of ADHD

Driven and built to invent, create, think outside the box, find similarities between disparate things, and to hyperfocus, the child with ADHD is wired for peak performance and success in the complicated and ever-changing twenty-first century.

When it comes to excelling at school or later in his career, match a child with ADHD with something that interests him and you'll likely wind up with a child that happily devotes hours to schoolwork without running out of steam or focus.

True, a child with ADHD may have problems focusing on things that are mundane and boring, such as where he put his pencils. But because his thinking process is different from that of other children, he has the sort of creative mindset that leads to great works of art, science, invention, a surplus of ideas, great enthusiasm and excitement, prolonged interest, and an ability to see the big picture, or see things in a holistic way.

RIGHT-BRAIN MASTERS
Children with ADHD also have the skills and right-brain power required to succeed in the twenty-first century. Because they thrive on

visual imagery and stimulation, they are naturally attracted to computers, which are accelerating the rate at which new information and knowledge can be disseminated and interrelated.

Because they tend to be less inhibited in their thinking, and more easily distracted by linear or logical thought, many children with ADHD are able to see connections and associations between seemingly disparate things. This accounts for their ability to think outside the box, come up with new solutions to old problems, piece together unrelated ideas or concepts, and create entirely new genres of art, music, writing, mathematics, etc.

Chronic disorganization and clutter are problems that are shared by most children with ADHD, however, many of them are highly adept at functioning in chaotic environments. In fact, they may actually require chaos to create, invent, or function at their peak. If you find yourself feeling overwhelmed by your chaotic environment, removing yourself from the situation for even just a few minutes can help you refocus and calm down.

NATURAL ENTREPRENEURS

Because children with ADHD are usually very eager to try something new, are highly intuitive and imaginative, and get the gist of things very quickly, they also grow up to make excellent entrepreneurs.

Studies show that children with ADHD turn into adults who are most effective and productive when they are their own bosses, or when they are allowed to work independently, at their own pace, and on their own time clocks. Mavericks by nature, children and adults with ADHD may not always be good followers, but they often excel as leaders.

If your child's school or teachers are stifling her creativity and motivation, consider looking for one that is flexible and open to dialogue, where your child will have some freedom to arrange her environment, schedule, and study habits.

Tapping Into Special Talents

The brain chemistry of children with ADHD differs from "normal" brains in its relationship to dopamine. As a result, children with ADHD crave stimulation just to feel alive.

Because of this craving, they are also more likely to seek thrills, take risks, discover new ways of doing things, act and think more boldly, stand out from the pack, and have a higher degree of personal charisma because they are bold, brave, and adventurous.

Your child may already have the raw material it takes to gain great fame and wealth. But why does the ADHD gene help a few people achieve outrageous success, while leaving many others struggling just to get by? Luck and chance always play some role, but the real secret may lie in your child understanding how to harness her innate strengths and minimize her ADHD weaknesses.

HARNESSING ADHD STRENGTHS

One of the most important things you can do to ensure your child's strengths have a chance to shine is to manage her ADHD symptoms consistently and effectively.

Make sure your child takes her medication regularly. Although medication alone can't fix poor grades in school, it can help your child manage mood swings and alleviate the restlessness, impulsivity, and inattention that may contribute to poor study habits.

The best treatment approach for most children with ADHD is a combination of medication, therapy, behavior modification, a healthy diet, regular exercise, support groups, relaxation techniques, and other lifestyle changes that enhance their lives.

HOW YOUR CHILD CAN MAKE ADHD WORK FOR HER

In addition to following her treatment program, encourage your child to turn many of her ADHD symptoms into assets by using the following tips and strategies:

- Encourage your child not to repress her ADHD gifts. Instead, have her look for ways to express her creativity, inventiveness, imagination, enthusiasm, and energy, at work, at home, and in social settings.

- Encourage your child to let her inattention be her guide. If she finds her mind constantly drifting and wandering, she shouldn't ignore the danger signs. Inattention can be a red flag that she's bored, disinterested, or unchallenged. ADHD can be the radar she needs to switch to a new line of study in school or college.

- Have your child make a list of her strengths and weaknesses, then match up her strengths and weaknesses to find out what sorts of jobs and careers are good matches.

- If your child doesn't know how to best use her ADHD skills, or if she's not even sure what they are, have her work with a career coach or therapist. Aptitude tests can help her home in on jobs and careers that would set her brain cells firing.

- Make sure your child understands that ambition alone is not enough to propel her to success. Many students with ADHD find it easy to get enthused about a new major in college, but aren't realistic about the time and effort required to get there. Help your child create a road map to get her from point A to point B, then encourage her to use her tremendous energy and drive to propel her down the road to success step-by-manageable-step.

- Encourage your child to use rather than abuse her innate ability to take risks. Harnessed properly, her ability to take a calculated leap of faith that would leave others teetering on the brink can be a tremendous asset. But taking careless or needless risks can set her back light years, and even endanger her physical or financial health. Make sure your child understands that before taking a leap, she should consider if it's worth the risk and whether she has a good chance of landing on solid ground.

O Have your child take inventory of her personal likes and dislikes to figure out what she wants to be. Does she like working on her feet in front of people (as a teacher does) or by herself in front of a computer (as a writer does)? If she's hyperactive, she might fare best in a job that lets her move around or that requires physical exertion, such as a sales job that gets her out and about, or a career that requires physical exertion, such as a personal fitness trainer.

O Tell your child not to stick with a line of study that doesn't match her personal profile just because she's worked extra hard to master it, or worked against some of her natural gifts or characteristics to be successful. Your child will be happier, less stressed, and more effective at a job that uses her natural gifts.

O Encourage your child to test drive another line of study if she doesn't like the one she's in. If her current major in college isn't using her imagination or creativity to the fullest, tell her to make arrangements to sit in on some classes she thinks she might enjoy more.

O Encourage your child to be patient with herself, and not to expect instant success if she decides to change course. Tell her she should prepare to spend some time examining her talents and skills, and talking with professionals to find a better match.

O Encourage your child to practice mindfulness to appreciate her gifts. Focusing on the positive aspects of her excess energy, creativity, and out-of-the-box thinking will help her be less judgmental of herself and her limitations.

THE IMPORTANCE OF OWNING UP

Many children with ADHD have become adept at masking their symptoms or covering them up with learned behavior. Although masking negative symptoms can certainly help life go more smoothly, if your child masks positive ADHD traits such as creativity, spontaneity, or thinking outside the box for fear of being "discovered," she could be sabotaging herself and limiting her ability to live life to the fullest.

If you and your child with ADHD are in denial about her symptoms, and/or you and she have been telling the world she's "normal" out of fear of social stigma, it may be time to let your child's ADHD genie out of the lamp. Your child's therapist can help you and your child "own" her positive ADHD traits and help her explore ways to use them to her best advantage.

Harnessing the Power of Friendship

Deciding whether or not to tell his friends he has ADHD could have a major effect on the way friends interact with and support your child, and it may also have an impact on feelings of trust.

If your child's symptoms are so mild that they don't interfere with his ability to make and keep friends, or if his symptoms are controlled by medication so that he is able to behave as a reliable and trustworthy friend, telling his friends he has ADHD is probably a decision he'll make on a case-by-case or need-to-know basis.

If his symptoms result in periodic moodiness, irritability, withdrawing, socially awkward behavior (such as putting his foot in his mouth), a tendency toward reckless behavior, impatience, restlessness, and so on, he may want to inform close friends of his disorder so they are more understanding of his symptoms. They'll be better able to put his ADHD-inspired idiosyncrasies into perspective and more forgiving when he says or does something inappropriate.

In fact, close friends in the know can help your child avoid embarrassing faux pas and help him function more effectively in social settings by acting as his personal interpreters when he can't follow a conversation, loses track of his thoughts, or is unable to read nonverbal cues or body language.

Friends who also have ADHD can help your child deal with the many challenges posed by the condition. Whether it's providing a safe place for him to rant about his symptoms, or providing him with ADHD information and ADHD resources, your child's ADHD friends can give him the sympathy, support, and empathy he needs to cope.

The Latest and Greatest ADHD Research

Although scientists have yet to find a cure for ADHD, sophisticated, high-tech research and equipment are shedding new light on what may cause or contribute to the disorder, and what types of treatments are most effective.

Many researchers now believe that ADHD is not one condition, but a cluster of conditions or disorders, each of which may be able to be treated. By discovering treatments for the individual conditions that make up ADHD, scientists one day hope to find an overall cure for the disorder.

The rapidly evolving technology of brain-imaging techniques is letting scientists observe how the brain functions when it has ADHD. By comparing such brains to brains without ADHD, researchers are finding distinctive differences in brain chemistry and makeup that categorize ADHD.

Scientists are hopeful that brain-imaging techniques can one day be used in the diagnosis and subsequent management of ADHD.

MATERNAL CONTRIBUTORS

Studies have also been conducted that have isolated how specific maternal factors cause or contribute to childhood ADHD. For instance, research indicates that mothers who smoke and drink alcohol during pregnancy are more likely to give birth to a child who develops ADHD.

In addition, new studies show that excessive maternal stress during pregnancy can contribute to a severe type of ADHD in children.

NEW DIRECTIONS IN RESEARCH

Researchers are studying the long-term effects of established ADHD treatments, such as medication, psychotherapy, and behavior modification, and are also looking at the long-term outcomes of children with ADHD who are not diagnosed or treated.

In addition, scientists are looking for safer and more effective medications to treat patients with ADHD alone, and with ADHD and coexisting conditions such as chronic anxiety, depression, and bipolar disorder.

Important Points to Consider

Having a child with ADHD can be a struggle, but there are also many wonderful moments you will be a part of during your child's life. It might not always be easy, but using conscious parenting techniques can help you recognize the positive and let go of the negative.

1. Remember that your child is unique and special. Your goal is to give her the tools to succeed in life.

2. You have a choice regarding how you react to your child and your surroundings.

3. When your initial inkling is to react with anger, try to take a moment and change your approach.

4. Forgive yourself for any mistakes, and allow yourself the room to learn from your past.

5. Practicing mindfulness techniques such as yoga, meditation, and deep breathing with your child can bring you closer together.

6. The emotional bond you have with your child is one of the most fulfilling parts of being a parent. Even when you are frustrated with your child, remind yourself how lucky you are to care as much as you do.

Index